Julius Caesar in Egypt

Julius Caesar in Egypt

Cleopatra and the War in Alexandria

Philip Matyszak

Pen & Sword
MILITARY

First published in Great Britain in 2023 by
Pen & Sword Military
An imprint of
Pen & Sword Books Ltd
Yorkshire – Philadelphia

Copyright © Philip Matyszak 2023

ISBN 978 1 39909 736 9

The right of Philip Matyszak to be identified as Author of this work has been asserted by him in accordance with the Copyright, Designs and Patents Act 1988.

A CIP catalogue record for this book is available from the British Library.

All rights reserved. No part of this book may be reproduced or transmitted in any form or by any means, electronic or mechanical including photocopying, recording or by any information storage and retrieval system, without permission from the Publisher in writing.

Typeset by Mac Style
Printed in the UK by CPI Group (UK) Ltd, Croydon, CR0 4YY.

Pen & Sword Books Limited incorporates the imprints of Atlas, Archaeology, Aviation, Discovery, Family History, Fiction, History, Maritime, Military, Military Classics, Politics, Select, Transport, True Crime, Air World, Frontline Publishing, Leo Cooper, Remember When, Seaforth Publishing, The Praetorian Press, Wharncliffe Local History, Wharncliffe Transport, Wharncliffe True Crime, White Owl and After the Battle.

For a complete list of Pen & Sword titles please contact

PEN & SWORD BOOKS LIMITED
47 Church Street, Barnsley, South Yorkshire, S70 2AS, England
E-mail: enquiries@pen-and-sword.co.uk
Website: www.pen-and-sword.co.uk

Or

PEN AND SWORD BOOKS
1950 Lawrence Rd, Havertown, PA 19083, USA
E-mail: Uspen-and-sword@casematepublishers.com
Website: www.penandswordbooks.com

Contents

Introduction		vi
Chapter 1	The Road to Alexandria – Gnaeus Pompey	1
Chapter 2	The Road to Alexandria – Cleopatra (the Seventh)	15
Chapter 3	The Road to Alexandria – Caius Julius Caesar	27
Chapter 4	Murder on the Nile	39
Chapter 5	Battleground Alexandria	57
Chapter 6	The Opening Rounds	69
Chapter 7	The War takes to the Water	81
Chapter 8	The Battle for Eunostos Harbour	93
Chapter 9	A Change of Management	113
Chapter 10	War Alongside the Nile	131
Chapter 11	The Final Showdown	143
Chapter 12	Aftermath	157
Chapter 13	Caesar in Alexandria – the Cultural Fallout	167
Index		173

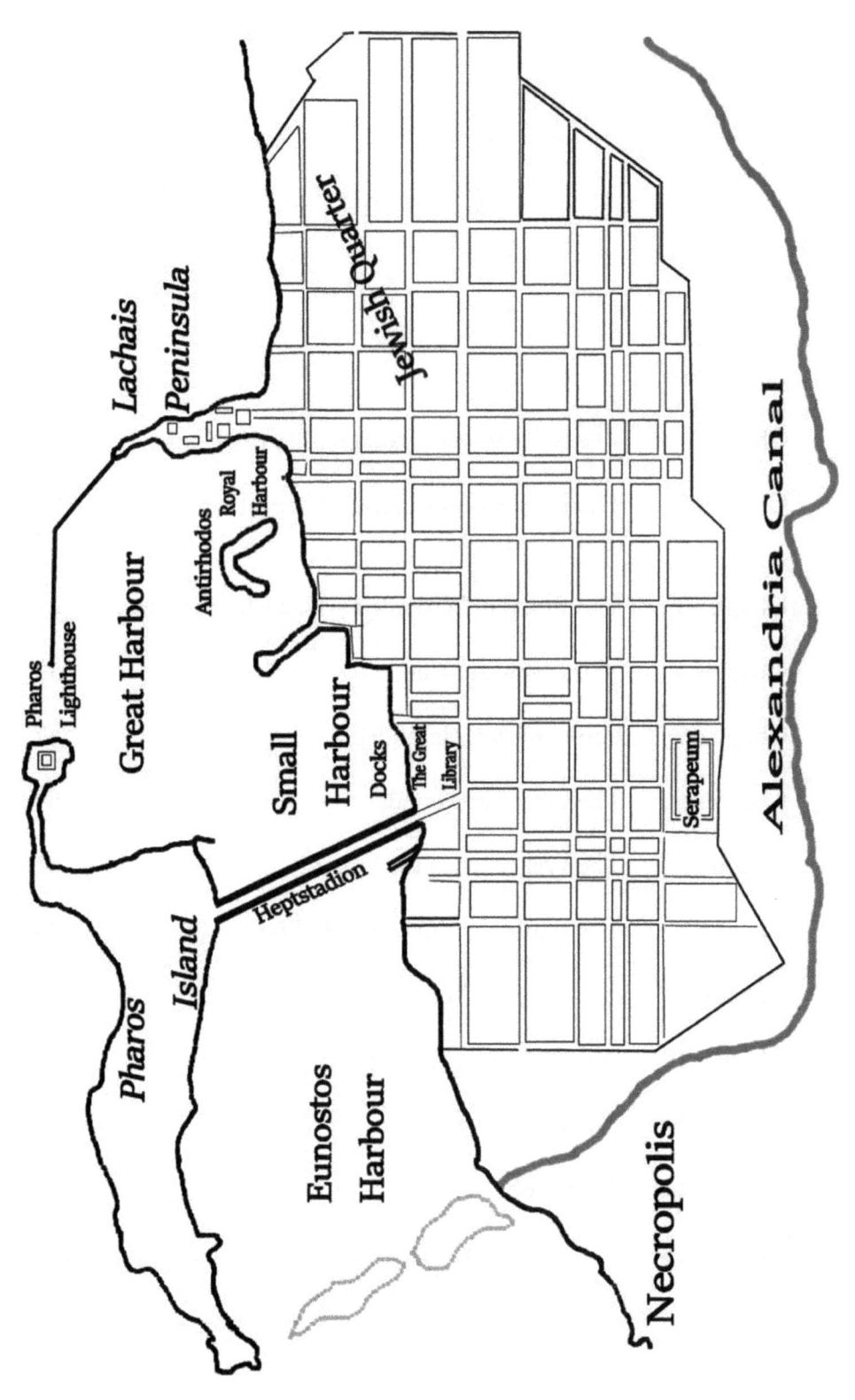

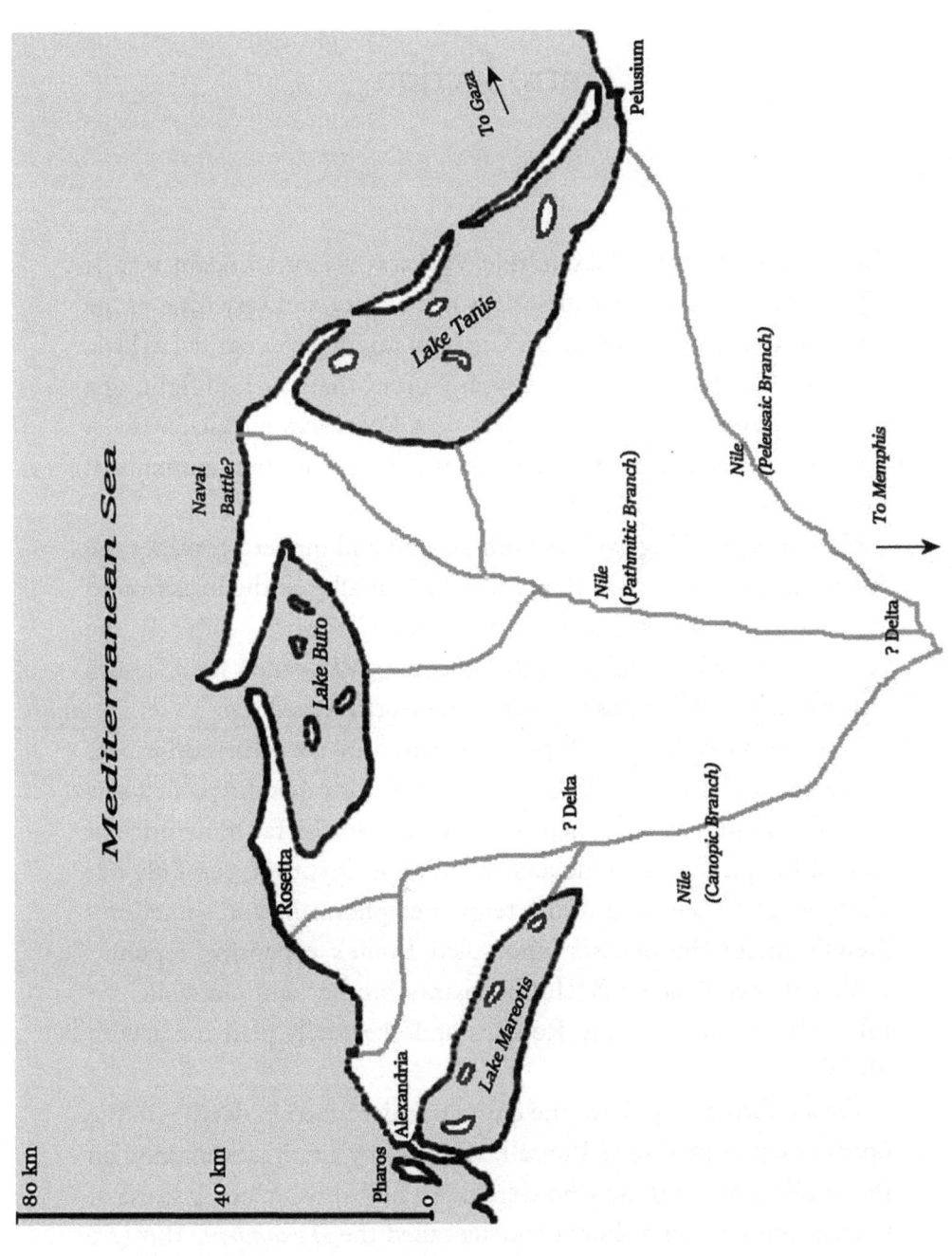

Introduction

In many ways the Alexandrian War was an insignificant war. It changed little of the course of world history, and very little of the history of Rome. Indeed, for Caesar it might have counted as little more than an incident on a four-year journey that saw him fighting a civil war across three continents (against Pharnaces in Asia, most of the Roman Republic in Europe, and the Egyptians and remnants of the Republican forces in Africa).

Generally speaking, writers both ancient and modern consider the Alexandrian War – when they consider it at all – as the background vehicle which allowed Caesar to meet Cleopatra, with all the ramifications which followed that meeting. Why then are Caesar's non-romantic adventures in Alexandria worth recording?

One reason is that for all practical purposes the Alexandrian war marks the fall of Ptolemaic Egypt – that historical oddity which saw a Greek kingdom established for 300 years in the far more ancient land of Egypt. The last independent ruler of Egypt was certainly not Cleopatra, who spent all of her reign metaphorically and sometimes literally under the dynasts who ruled Rome's collapsing republic. Rather it was Ptolemy XIII, Cleopatra's brother and erstwhile co-ruler who stood up to the Romans and eventually paid for it with his life.

We are fortunate to have the entire war described in detail – in the opening weeks by Caesar himself, and later by a writer who drew on the recollections of those who were there, probably including those of Caesar himself – in a short excursus called the *Alexandrine War* (*De Bello Alexandrino*).

As with any ancient text, the *Alexandrine War* must be examined carefully for bias, because it was at best written with implicit bias by a Caesarian supporter, and at worse by that supporter as a piece of outright propaganda. Since Caesar does not come out of a reading of the *Alexandrine War* particularly well, one can only speculate what sort of character he would have made in a text written by someone on the opposing side.

It is partly because the *Alexandrine War* is a biased account of events during that short but nasty war that the story demands re-telling by a more neutral narrator, but also because the *Alexandrine War* does not tell the full story. Indeed, to some extent the full story could not be told until recently due to the partial absence of one of the main characters of the tale – Cleopatra's Alexandria.

For centuries Alexandria was a frustrating wasteland to archaeologists who knew very well that the remains of one of the greatest cities of antiquity lay somewhere under the modern metropolis – if they simply could discover where much of it had gone. It turns out that they were looking in the wrong place. Many of the sites described in the contemporary texts were still there – sometimes in rather good condition – but at the bottom of the harbour rather than under the streets of Alexandria.

These remains were discovered in the nick of time before the modern world destroyed them completely. At the time of the discovery of Cleopatra's palace the harbour authorities were about to drop 50-ton lumps of concrete on it to form a breakwater. Today, not only are a wonderful array of artefacts emerging into the light after millennia underwater, but also the geography described by Caesar's narrators is starting to make sense.

There is another reason for re-visiting the Alexandrian war and that is because the ancient text does indeed treat the war as an incident on a journey. It was written within a few years of the epic struggle of the civil war. If the writer/editor was the Caesarian consul Hirtius, then he perished within five years of the events he was describing. At that distance in time not only is it hard for a writer to distinguish the wood from the trees but the writer naturally takes it for granted that the reader is equally familiar with the world-shaking events before and immediately afterwards.

That, in order to put things in context, readers might need a quick summary of who Gnaeus Pompey was, or what happened at the Battle of Pharsalus, is not something that would have occurred to Hirtius or any other contemporary writer. However, this kind of background briefing is certainly necessary for the general reader 2,000 years later. It is now necessary to explain where and how the Alexandrian War fitted into the more general chaos of Caesar's civil war, and why events elsewhere had a dramatic effect in Caesar's ability to wage war in Alexandria.

A re-visit to the war can now also be somewhat more comprehensive in another sense. As well as the additional input of archaeology, we also have details and perspectives from later writers of the Roman imperial era who were even more deeply interested in Julius Caesar than we are today. Caesar's biographer Plutarch gives us additional details of the war, and plenty more detail on Cleopatra – who rather embarrassed Caesar and the writer of the *Alexandrine War*, both of whom therefore tend to shunt the lady to the sidelines of their accounts.

It is uncertain how details of Rome's leader canoodling with an Egyptian queen might have gone down with the contemporary Roman public of 44 BC – especially as that queen had spent the last year of Caesar's life camped out in the suburbs of Rome demanding recognition for the son they had conceived together. However, the Romans would certainly have been unimpressed to find that Caesar's sex drive had led to an unnecessary war and a substantial loss of Roman lives. Yet Plutarch, writing a century later, can happily dish the dirt without fear of a political backlash. His version of events is rounded off by the work of an even-later historian, Cassius Dio, who wrote some time around AD 200. Between these and mentions in the texts of other ancient authors such as Appian and Josephus we get a more rounded picture of what happened in Alexandria and why.

A final reason for describing what happened in the Alexandrian war is because of what it tells us about Julius Caesar himself. This war saw Caesar at his best and worst. The best is Caesar the military commander. Stuck in an unenviable position, surrounded by an army that greatly outnumbered his own, in a city whose inhabitants loathed his very being, Caesar acted coolly and precisely. In any war there will be military missteps (blamed, as always in Caesarian texts, upon over-enthusiastic or incompetent subordinates) but Caesar recovered from these with easy expertise, though one particularly catastrophic misjudgement almost cost him his life.

We see Caesar stand off his enemies, counter-attack with economical precision, and take crucial decisions regardless of the cost. It was Caesar rather than his opponents who burned the fleet with which the Romans could have escaped from Alexandria. Yet had Caesar not done so he might have lost the war and his life. All the while, Caesar kept up the morale of his men, who never gave him less than a hundred per cent when a lesser commander would have certainly suffered their opprobrium for getting them into that mess in the first place.

Which brings us to the worst of Julius Caesar. The main charge against Caesar is that the Alexandrian war, with the thousands of lives lost on both sides, need never have happened. With his usual impetuosity Caesar rushed into Egypt with what turned out to be unnecessary haste. That might not have been foreseeable, but the result of that haste was that Caesar brought with him totally inadequate forces. ('He brought too many men for a diplomatic embassy, too few for an army' as Tigranes of Armenia remarked of a similar move by Caesar's contemporary Lucullus.)

Once Caesar found himself outnumbered in hostile territory he needed all his diplomatic and political skill to extricate himself. Yet this was a man whose diplomatic inability had caused the Roman aristocracy to declare war upon him, the man whose inability to counter the machinations of Vercingetorix led to a rebellion that almost cost him Gaul, and who ended his life being stabbed to death on the Senate floor by his alienated contemporaries. Given that record, we need not be surprised that Caesar comprehensively botched the diplomatic situation in Alexandria. When he arrived, the Alexandrians were desperate to see him leave. Within a matter of months they were blockading their harbour in order to keep him in town so that they could kill him. Caesar could have that effect on people.

It is therefore necessary in this text to chart the series of diplomatic missteps which led the Egyptian army and the people of Alexandria to declare war on Caesar, since without an understanding of how Caesar brought the war upon himself the war itself cannot be understood. Nor, among these missteps, should we underestimate the extent to which Caesar's sexual involvement with Cleopatra was a diplomatic *faux pas*.

In some ways, from the moment he arrived in the country, Caesar could not have behaved much differently if he had come to Egypt with the intention all along of provoking the Egyptians and the townsfolk of Alexandria into starting a war. Yet this begs the question of why, if that had been his intention, he did not bring with him an army with which to fight that war. Or indeed, why he ordered the disbandment of the army of the only potential ally currently capable of fighting that war for him. The only answer is that Caesar did not really intend to go to war. He had very little experience of diplomacy (or need for it) in his military career to date. He therefore mismanaged the situation into a war, at which fortunately he had a great deal of experience.

The story of the Alexandrian War is in fact the story of Caesar using his considerable military prowess to get himself out of a situation which should have never arisen in the first place. As will be seen, had he really wanted only to instal Cleopatra in power, a quick visit with the force of the Roman army behind him could have accomplished this later without the loss of thousands of lives. As it was, an ad hoc decision taken just when the political situation was finely balanced had catastrophic consequences. This book, therefore, is a detailed exploration of how Caesar stumbled into his Alexandrian adventure, how his sojourn in Alexandria almost got him killed, and how his military genius got him out of it – with the help of his loyal legionaries. Had Caesar brought lesser men with him to Egypt he certainly would not have come home alive.

As mentioned earlier, the story of the Alexandrian War is also but a single chapter in the larger story of Caesar's civil war with the senatorial faction of the Roman Republic. Therefore we must start by placing the Alexandrian War in context and examining the complex backstory of how Caesar, that fateful autumn of 48 BC, happened to be in Alexandria in the first place.

Chapter 1

The Road to Alexandria – Gnaeus Pompey

What do you do if you are the greatest general in the world, yet you can't fight battles? This was the problem which faced Gnaeus Pompeius Magnus, the man known today as Pompey the Great. And when it came to soldiering, 'great' Pompey certainly was.

For almost a century the Mediterranean had been plagued by pirates who had not only disrupted grain supplies and pillaged merchant ships but had even raided coastal cities, the most blatant attack being on the port of Ostia just a few miles from Rome. Repeated attempts by different Roman commanders to control the menace had all failed, until finally the exasperated Roman people had given the job to Pompey (along with unprecedented powers to get the job done). Despite occasional sabotage by jealous senatorial rivals, Pompey succeeded in clearing the Mediterranean of pirates in a single season.

Pompey went on to defeat Mithridates of Pontus, a king who had challenged Rome for decades, and then went on to campaign in Syria, where he settled the chaotic situation that had followed the collapse of the Hellenistic Seleucid kingdom. Yet in all this series of victorious military campaigns, Pompey never fought a single significant battle.

As a young man Pompey had learned the hard way that he was not very good at battles. While campaigning in Spain against the province's rebel governor, Quintus Sertorius, Pompey had initially been full of youthful confidence. This faded fast after a series of engagements from which the wily and experienced Sertorius generally emerged the winner. ('Spanking the schoolboy' was how Sertorius described it.) At best, Pompey emerged from these clashes with his army partly intact, at worst he was soundly defeated. The young general got the message. Battles were uncertain affairs in which small elements could have major effects, and victory was but a hair's breadth away from defeat. Far better then, not to fight battles at all.

Pompey could avoid battles because he was a very, very good general. His frustrated enemies found thereafter that Pompey always occupied the better position with more men so that any attack on him would be suicidal. Yet at the same time Pompey's mastery of logistics meant that his armies were well-fed and supplied while his opponents starved. When things did come to a final confrontation, the result was either a one-sided walkover or the bloodless surrender of the outmanoeuvred and outnumbered foe.

In Spain Sertorius was assassinated by Perpenna, his second-in-command, whom Pompey immediately set about isolating and then cornering. In 72 BC Perpenna, knowing that all was lost, challenged Pompey to a final all-or-nothing battle. For over a week Pompey held off before ordering his men to retreat. The exultant Perpenna followed up and promptly marched his army into a carefully-prepared trap. The subsequent engagement was less of a battle than an ambush, rout and massacre. This triumphant end to the war in Spain confirmed what Pompey had repeatedly told anyone who would listen – that he was indeed a great general.

In the years and campaigns since, Pompey never fought a major battle, yet repeatedly secured victory for Rome. So great was his reputation that by 49 BC it was quite predictable that the aristocrats of the Roman Senate, when they needed a champion to lead them against the renegade general Julius Caesar, would turn to Pompey.

While a great general, Pompey was at best a mediocre politician. He and the Roman Senate had badly underestimated Caesar's popularity with the common people of Italy. In fact Pompey had once boasted of his own popularity: 'If I stamp my foot, Italy will rise.' And indeed Pompey stamped, and Italy rose – against him. By and large the people of Italy were tired of endless civil strife and saw no need to fight for a corrupt and selfish Senate that cared little for their interests. So when Pompey rashly declared that anyone who was not for his side was against it, most of Italy became Caesarian by default.

Politically, Pompey was often out of his depth, but if bad politics had cost him Italy, militarily he was still on top of the situation and immediately grasped what he had to do next. Caesar had swept through Italy with his veteran army, and the troops Pompey had called upon had either declined to answer his summons or were green, untrained recruits. If the Senate could not hold Italy, then Italy would have to be abandoned. Pompey ordered an immediate retreat to Greece, knowing that there he could summon aid from his client kings in the East and from the Roman garrisons stationed there.

In Greece Pompey consolidated his forces and set about doing what he did best – defeating the enemy without a battle. Caesar discovered how difficult an opponent he was facing when he engaged with Pompey at the port of Dyrrhachium. Though the senatorial army had superior numbers, Pompey's men were outmatched by Caesar's veterans, so Pompey avoided a direct confrontation. Instead, he played a wily game in which Caesar was gradually outmanoeuvred and his forces eventually routed. Later Caesar reckoned that during that precipitate retreat bold use by Pompey of his cavalry could have crushed the Caesarian army – 'They would have won, had their leader not been a loser' (Plutarch, *Pompey* 65).

Yet Caesar did not see the bigger picture. A consummate risk-taker himself, he could not understand that Pompey had held back his cavalry because there were risks involved, and Pompey saw no need to take risks. Pompey had the measure of his enemy and could take his time. Thereafter, as Plutarch puts it, 'Pompey set out in pursuit of Caesar, determined to avoid a battle but to keep his enemy hard-pressed and short of supplies' (Plutarch, *Pompey* 67). This he did so successfully that Caesar complained that he was not fighting men but shortages and hunger. So bad did things become that at one point

4 Julius Caesar in Egypt

Caesar could only offer his legionaries the dubious culinary benefits of bread baked from grass.

Basically, at this point Caesar's war had ended and he was defeated. Greece is a mountainous country with little agricultural land. There is a reason why most campaigns in that country had heretofore involved armies of fewer than 20,000 men – a commander simply could not feed more than that number without supplies being brought in from abroad. Pompey had around 45,000 men, who were well fed with corn from Asia Minor and Egypt. Caesar had around 22,000 men who had to live off the land – and they were starving.

Needing to feed his troops, Caesar made a break for northern Thessaly with Pompey patiently dogging his heels, using his superior strength in cavalry to ensure that Caesar's men could not spread out to forage. Eventually, somewhere near the town of Pharsalus, Caesar found a fertile valley and was forced to take his hungry army there to pillage whatever was available.

Pompey had no reason to be dissatisfied with this. It was now August in the time between the harvest and the sowing of new crops, so Caesar's legions would soon exhaust the food in their temporary sanctuary. All Pompey had to do was guard the exit to the valley, ensure that Caesar could not ford the nearby Enipeus River and let starvation win the war for him.

Militarily Pompey had matters well under control. He was very good at things military. Politically however, the situation was spiralling out of control. In his campaign Pompey had not factored in the very thing which had been a major cause of the civil war in the first place – the arrogance, incompetence and blind stupidity of the Roman Senate.

When Caesar had conquered Italy and Rome, the majority of these senators had fled the city to Pompey's camp. These men were eager to return to Rome and had little patience with Pompey's patient and careful campaign. They had enough military ability between them to know that Caesar had been on the ropes at Dyrrhachium, and they could not understand why Pompey had let his opponent get away on that occasion. The only explanation that they could see was that Pompey was prolonging the war to increase his personal power – that was, after all, what most of them would have done given the chance.

It was widely rumoured in the army that, once Caesar had been disposed of, the Senate intended the over-mighty Pompey to be next. Many thought that Pompey had doubtless heard those rumours and was consequently hanging on to his command to avoid that fateful day. Since Caesar was all but beaten, it seemed to the senators that one last push would be enough to finish a war that was already won. Already, top senators such as Scipio and Domitius Ahenobarbus were squabbling and scheming over which of them should take over from Caesar as Pontifex Maximus.

The result was that Pompey faced something of a mutiny – at his next council of war senator after senator stood up and demanded that Caesar be immediately crushed in battle. If the senatorial side offered a confrontation, there was no doubt that Caesar would accept. To get out of the trap he was in he wanted – needed – a battle. For days he had been edging his men closer and closer to the hill where Pompey's legions were encamped, hoping to entice the enemy to leave this advantageous position and engage him on the level plain. Pompey, naturally, had disdained Caesar's provocation without realizing how this must look to the other senators who daily saw the chance to finish the war dangled before them.

So now Pompey had to risk everything in a battle he did not want and did not need. Furthermore, he was aware – with an awareness bordering on panic – that both Caesar and his veteran army were very good at fighting battles, and he was not. Nor was his army, which was mostly reluctant levies and raw recruits. The Pompeians could hold off Caesar's legionaries, but only if securely established in an advantageous position. However, Pompey had grave – and justified – doubts as to how his troops would perform in combat on even terms.

We have detailed accounts of the battle from two perspectives. Pompey's biographer, Plutarch, writing just over a century after Pompey's death, gives an account of events from the point of view of the senatorial side. The other narrator wrote soon after the battle. He necessarily gives us the perspective from Caesar's side, because he was in fact, Julius Caesar.

In his text, today called *The Civil Wars,* Caesar explains that he had given up attempting to force Pompey to fight. That morning he was planning to force his way out of the valley to find fresh fields to plunder, his hopes of survival being based on the hope that Pompey's men would eventually tire of chasing him. Caesar had already prepared his army for the move when it was observed that Pompey's army had advanced into the plain and was actually offering battle. Caesar downplays the incredulous delight he must have felt, though Plutarch assures us that the Caesarian army observed this development with 'shouts of joy'.

One of the key elements of the battlefield was the River Enipeus, upon which both armies anchored one flank. Since it was impossible for either army to be outflanked on that side, cavalry and light infantry were concentrated on the other flank of both armies (Caesar's right flank and Pompey's left).

It was clear to both commanders that the action on that flank would be critical. Pompey intended to use his superior cavalry to smash through Caesar's defences on that side, while Caesar, fully aware of the peril, thinned his battle line in order to have extra reserves available on the endangered flank. The existence of these reserves was hidden from Pompey by the Caesarian cavalry, which screened them from view.

Pompey's battle plan went like this. As the two sides moved across the valley floor towards each other, Pompey's cavalry would advance *en masse* ahead of the main army and close on Caesar's right flank. There they would wait for Caesar's legions to charge at the Pompeian army. There was an established pattern to such charges. When they came within range, the legionaries would let fly with their heavy throwing spears (*pila*) and then charge into contact. On this occasion though, Pompey had decided to change the script. To give his cavalry more time to work around the Caesarian flank and to pull the Caesarian army further out of position, Pompey had ordered his men not to countercharge the Caesarian line but to take the attack standing still.

This would also help Pompey's less experienced soldiers hold formation, while their greater numbers could absorb the impact of Caesar's charge (Pompey had 40,000 men to Caesar's 22,000). Furthermore, since Caesar's soldiers were expecting a countercharge that wasn't going to happen, they would have to run twice the expected distance – in full armour – and arrive at the Pompeian front ranks winded and disorganized. They would also be some distance ahead of where Caesar would expect them to be, and this would expose Caesar's right flank even more.

Even before the Caesarian line had completed its charge, the Pompeian cavalry was intended to hit Caesar's right flank like a thunderbolt and roll back the numerically weaker horsemen opposing them. Ideally, the stationary and rested Pompeian legionaries would engage with the breathless and somewhat confused Caesarian legionaries just as the Pompeian cavalry hit those legionaries from behind. The Caesarian line would break and the battle would become a massacre. Or it would, had not Pompey been fighting Caesar and Caesar's battle-hardened army.

Pompey had taken position on his left wing personally to oversee the crucial attack of Caesar's right flank. From this post he was in an excellent position to see his battle strategy crumble into ruins as Caesar's army nullified each of his tactics in turn.

Firstly, the Caesarian legionaries did not charge headlong into the waiting Pompeian battle-line. When the charging legionaries had got halfway toward the enemy and realized that no countercharge was coming, the veteran soldiers spontaneously halted and re-dressed their lines. Then, when they were again organized and breathing easily, they charged across the remaining distance and threw themselves upon their stationary enemy.

Meanwhile Pompey's 6,000 cavalry hurtled down upon Caesar's right flank, where less than a sixth of that number of Caesarian horsemen awaited them. As expected, the Caesarian cavalry melted away in the face of the Pompeian attack. At this point the Pompeian cavalry expected to see the exposed backs of Caesar's legionaries as those legionaries engaged the Pompeian battle-line. Instead, they were confronted by the organized ranks of the infantry whom Caesar had pulled out of the main line for just this purpose.

As the Pompeian cavalry advance stalled in the face of this unexpected threat, the Caesarians charged. Cavalry caught standing by an infantry charge are somewhat vulnerable, and Caesar's legionaries made things worse by using their *pila* as stabbing spears, jabbing the long weapons up at the faces and unprotected thighs of the horsemen. Then, while the Pompeian cavalry were still reeling from this unexpected assault, the Caesarian cavalry charged back into the fray with exquisite timing and their unexpected attack broke their numerically superior enemy.

Pompey watched with dismay as his cavalry were routed and a mass of Caesarian cavalry and heavy infantry smashed through the light infantry and archers with whom he had intended to follow up his cavalry's success. Now it was Pompey's flank which was exposed. It did not take a brilliant general to see what was going to happen next, though being a brilliant general – as Pompey was – probably helped in foreseeing forthcoming developments with crystal clarity.

The struggle on the river flank and in the centre was deadlocked, with the skill of Caesar's more-experienced fighters balanced by the sheer numbers of the opposition. Yet the morale of Pompey's army was fragile (as was the morale of Pompey himself). Once Caesar's outflanking forces hit the troops fighting in the centre, then that part of Pompey's army would buckle, especially as Caesar could be counted upon to throw his reserves against the centre at the critical moment.

(He did.) That would leave only the soldiers on the river flank still fighting, and they could hardly be expected to hold out while their comrades were quite literally heading for the hills.

A different general might have charged down to the centre and tried to pull men from the back of his battle-line to hold off the outflanking enemy. After all, given his superior numbers, Pompey had men to spare. Perhaps, given inspired leadership, the Pompeian side might yet win the day. Yet on the day the leadership was not inspired. Instead, it was gloomily despairing. One suspects that Pompey knew his own ability when it came to fighting battles, and in the end things had gone pretty much as badly as he had always suspected they would. The dejected Pompey abandoned his army to its inevitable fate and rode back to his camp. There he planned to wait in his tent until news arrived of the expected disaster.

The news, when it came, was borne not by messengers but by Caesar's legionaries. These, by ripping into the camp's defenders, testified that the main battle was already over. Pompey's camp garrison fought ferociously in a doomed cause and again Pompey did not wait to discover the outcome of the struggle. Instead, he carefully removed his insignia of office and slipped out of the camp during the chaos – just one more confused citizen among many.

Now, with only a few retainers for company, Pompey's task was to remain ahead of the Caesarian army which sought him as the main prize of their victory. Pompey knew that Caesar would be preoccupied with re-organizing his army and accommodating a huge number of prisoners. There was also the matter of dealing with the huge number of Pompeian troops who had fled the battlefield, rallied on nearby hilltops and were now forlornly waiting for orders.

From Caesar's point of view it was essential that those orders came from him rather than the remnants of the Pompeian command. Already, for example, Pompey's competent subordinate Cato was gathering as much of the shattered army as he could and leading them towards the coast. Those men whom Caesar encountered he lured from their defensive positions with promises of mercy – which he kept. Not only were the prisoners well treated but Caesar instructed his legionaries to refrain from helping themselves to the property of the prisoners. This was effective and encouraged further surrenders, but it also distracted Caesar and allowed Pompey to get a head start on his run to the coast.

Pompey headed east through the Vale of Tempe in Thessaly, and lightened the small entourage he had picked up on his flight by instructing the servants to leave him and make their peace with Caesar. He himself boarded a riverboat and so made his way to the coast. From there Pompey crossed to the island of Lesbos where his wife was waiting at Mytilene with a small garrison and part of the Pompeian cash reserve.

The immediate crisis was over. Caesar had suspected that Pompey would do rather as he himself would have done – which was head north to Macedonia and attempt to rally the garrison there. As the Romans knew from bitter experience in their wars against Philip V of Macedon, once an army was guarding the mountain passes between Greece and Macedonia, it was very hard for an invader to gain access. However, Pompey had not gone north but abandoned the mainland altogether. The time it took for Caesar to realize this gave Pompey time to consider his next move.

His current location of Lesbos was somewhat too close for comfort to mainland Greece, so Pompey and those who had managed to rejoin him adjourned to Cilicia in southern Anatolia. There followed a council of war at which there was general agreement that, while Pharsalus had been a devastating blow, it might yet prove not to have been a decisive one. As the historian Cassius Dio remarked:

> Had he taken the right steps perhaps he could have recovered everything. A substantial part of his army had survived and the other forces at his disposal were not trivial. He still had a

substantial war chest, and his fleet dominated the sea. Even in his misfortune cities there and in Asia Minor were loyal to him.

(Cassius Dio, *History* 42.1)

Cato had assembled a moderately substantial army from the remnants of the force that had fled Pharsalus. He had taken this force in the opposite direction to Pompey's flight, and was at Corcyra rallying as many men there as he could. Later he would sail with this army to the province of Africa (modern Tunisia), which still held out against Caesar. Spain was once another Pompeian stronghold and, indeed, unbeknownst to Pompey, his sons Gnaeus and Sextus were already on their way there to raise the peninsula in arms against Caesar. Italy had surrendered quickly to the Caesareans, but Caesar had now been away from Italy for some time, and the Italians were growing restless.

Meanwhile on the other side of Anatolia, in Pontus – another region conquered by Pompey – there was a further distraction awaiting Caesar's attention. King Pharnaces II was eager to restore his former kingdom's lost glory. While Pharnaces was no friend to Pompey, he was an enemy of Rome to whom Caesar had to give some attention lest he be accused of pursuing his civil war while Rome's empire collapsed around him.

Also, there was the fleet. Last time anyone had checked, the Roman fleet was still loyal to Pompey, which was why Pompey had been able to supply his army from Egypt and Asia Minor while Caesar was feeding his soldiers bread baked from grass.

In other words, all was not lost. Apart from anything else, the senatorial side still had Pompey himself – a general who had fared disastrously at Pharsalus, but who was still better at strategy and logistics than anyone else in the known world. If Caesar's many enemies could choose one man who could combine their far-flung assets into a coherent whole and effectively wield them as an effective fighting force, the best man for the job would still be the man they had: Pompey.

So what Pompey now needed was to direct the war from a secure base where he could rally the still-powerful forces scattered by the Pharsalian debacle. This needed to be somewhere which allowed effective control of resources in provinces from Spain to Syria to Africa.

One refuge that could be immediately ruled out was the Parthian empire to the east. Plutarch, who was a much better biographer than he was military strategist, feels that Pompey should have headed east across the Euphrates. With perfect hindsight he speculated that some 'evil spirit' had instead guided Pompey to his doom. Yet there were numerous reasons for not choosing Parthia – and not merely the risk (says Plutarch) of Pompey's wife getting ravished by the cruel and lascivious barbarians.

Contemporary Parthia was something of a *bete noire* for the Romans. Less than a decade previously the Roman triumvir Licinius Crassus had tried to conquer that kingdom with a massive and disastrous invasion that had cost Rome some thirty thousand men. The Parthians were still more than somewhat bitter about that unprovoked invasion and knew that Pompey had been closely associated with Crassus. Indeed, when Pompey had sent an envoy asking for Parthian help, the Parthian response had been to throw the messenger – a Roman senator – into the dungeons.

If Arsaces, the Parthian king, took in Pompey, it would be because Arsaces wanted a subordinate puppet to use against Rome – as Caesarian propaganda would endlessly point out. Furthermore, the Parthian capital east of the Euphrates was far from being the ideal centre for coordinating resistance to Caesar, resistance which would in the first instance be concentrated in Africa and Spain.

Ideally Pompey needed a place that had excellent lines of communication, was secure from attack and where he would be the person in charge. That place was Egypt. The present pharaoh of Egypt was Ptolemy XIII, a ruler just entering into his teens and deeply indebted to Pompey for aid that Pompey had given to his father Ptolemy XII Auletes.

Egypt had suffered centuries of misrule under the decayed Ptolemaic dynasty, yet the country was still rich. It was bordered by sea and desert, so, unless Caesar wanted the tough job of fighting his way in through Gaza, he could only approach Egypt by ship – and Pompey retained hopes that his fleet could control the seas. The Egyptian capital of Alexandria was only two weeks sail from Rome, and once Pompeian forces had secured Cyrenaica, the southern Mediterranean would be under their control. Furthermore, though nominally independent, Egypt had been subordinate to Rome for decades and Egyptian courtiers and bureaucrats were accustomed to Romans calling the shots.

In short then, if Pompey and his wife fled eastwards they could probably find sanctuary in Parthia and live out their lives as political pawns in a gilded prison. But Pompey would be admitting that his cause was lost and that he had abandoned Rome. This was simply not going to happen. Pompey was a Roman, and like most Romans of his generation he possessed a particular form of stubbornness that went well beyond obstinacy into a bloody-minded refusal to back down and accept defeat, or indeed even to accept reality. Pompey had lost at Pharsalus because the Senate had forced him to fight a battle he had known he was going to lose. That did not mean Pompey was beaten. He was going to fight back, and that fightback would start in Egypt.

Chapter 2

The Road to Alexandria – Cleopatra (the Seventh)

Contemporary Egypt was ideal in many ways from the point of view of a defeated Roman general looking to wrest back control of the Roman empire from a usurper. That is not to say however, that Egypt itself was in great shape. One might say that it was indicative of the condition of the country that the uncle of the current pharaoh was also the current ruler's father, and furthermore the same uncle was the pharaoh's father-in-law as well.

There is some debate as to whether Egypt's Ptolemaic line of pharaohs had degenerated into chaos as a result of generations of incestuous brother-sister marriage, but intense inbreeding probably did not help. Certainly, it did not help the country itself, where dynastic infighting had caused the Ptolemies to rack up huge debts, payments for which were now being squeezed from the country's unfortunate taxpayers. Adding to the general misery in contemporary Egypt, the political situation had now deteriorated into (yet another) civil war. To understand the situation in Egypt on the arrival of Rome's warring dynasts one has to look back several generations to before the original conquest of the country by Alexander the Great.

Even before Pompey arrived in Egypt, the land was already ancient. To get some idea of how ancient consider the country's calendar. This calendar had 365 days, but no leap year. Consequently, every four years the calendar moved back a day relative to the solar year. (i.e. in modern terms, January 1 happened on 31 December and four years later on 30 December, and so on.) By the time of Pompey's arrival in

Alexandria that missing day had moved backwards through the entire Egyptian calendar – twice.

In earlier millennia Egypt had dominated the civilized world with pharaohs such as Ramesses II leading campaigns up through the Levant as far as Damascus. Egypt was one of the world's first and greatest centres of civilization, and the Egyptians were very proud of that fact. As a people who thought of themselves as conquerors rather than the conquered, the Egyptians had been hugely humiliated when the Persians had defeated and taken their nation in 525 BC. Thereafter, Egypt's unfortunate Persian governors had been forced to deal with successive waves of nationalist uprisings.

Then Alexander the Great had attacked the Persians and taken over Egypt. To demonstrate that Egypt was now part of the Greek world, in 331 BC Alexander founded the most successful of the many cities named after himself, Alexandria on the Nile. On Alexander's death, Egypt was taken over by one of his generals, a man called Ptolemy, the founder of Egypt's Ptolemaic dynasty.

Thenceforth Egypt had even more of a split personality. (The country already had a pronounced split between the more conservative south and the – relatively – cosmopolitan north.) Egypt's new Greek rulers did not try to recreate their new possession as a Greek state. Certainly some new Greek cities with Greek immigrants sprang up in the Egyptian interior, but these were generally self-sufficient islands in an Egyptian sea. For most of rural Egypt life under Greek rule went on as it had done in the preceding centuries and in the millennia before that. The population was mainly agricultural, and the pattern of people's lives was determined by the seasonal rise of the Nile. The river flooded the low-lying nearby fields, depositing silt which led to the rich harvests which were the foundation of the country's wealth.

To a very large extent Egypt was a theocracy with the priestly caste dominant in the administration. Despite successive changes at the top, this administration had not changed much for centuries, for Egypt's new rulers were not interested in changing the system, but merely putting themselves on top if it. Thus when the Greek general Ptolemy took over Egypt, he immediately promoted himself to Pharaoh and proceeded to behave towards his Egyptian subjects as though he and his family had been Egyptian Pharaohs forever. Even today statues and bas-reliefs show Ptolemy in Egyptian dress, with the traditional Egyptian symbols of rank, giving due deference to the gods (and by implication, the priestly administrators) of Egypt.

Yet if the Ptolemy who faced southwards into the Egyptian interior attempted to out-Egyptian the Egyptians, the Ptolemy who faced outward into the Mediterranean world tried to show that he was more Greek than the Greeks. The showcase for Greek Egypt was Alexandria, which Ptolemy and his successor Ptolemy II built into the greatest and most populous city in the known world. This was a metropolis which in every way was in a totally different league to, for example, the somewhat shabby and culturally backward capital of the Roman state which was at that time coming to dominate the Italian peninsula.

For most of the first and second century BC, Alexandria was the centre of the Greek world, far outshining even Athens, which never recovered from Macedonian conquest to regain the heights it had attained in the age of Pericles. It was to Alexandria that poets and philosophers came in search of patrons, here that some of the greatest scientific discoveries of the age were made. Here Euclid wrote his 'Principles of Geometry' and Eratosthenes (accurately) calculated the circumference of the earth.

Egypt dominated the neighbouring state of Cyrenaica and extended its power far into the Aegean sea. Cyprus, briefly occupied by Egypt in the sixth century BC, came again under Egyptian control under the Ptolemies, as did many of the nearby islands. Under the Ptolemies Cyprus became not Egyptian but thoroughly Greek, with the Greek alphabet replacing the native script and worship of Greek gods replacing native cults. In Egypt itself one of the most enduring legacies of the Ptolemies was that the need to transport goods from the Red Sea to the Mediterranean led the Ptolemies to import a hardy species of pack animal from central Asia. That animal, the camel, is now so integral to life in North Africa that it is practically emblematic of the region.

Camels were needed for transport because the Ptolemies worked hard and successfully to make Alexandria the trade hub of the eastern Mediterranean. In part Egypt's rulers were able to do this because Egypt's first Greek ruler, Alexander the Great, had demolished the previous trade hub – the city of Tyre – so comprehensively that it was generations before the site rose to be more than a mere village.

It was to Egypt that ships were carried westward by the trade winds from India and these ships carried silks and spices from even further east. Many of these goods were repackaged in Alexandria for export along with gold and ivory from the African interior, but much also remained in Alexandria for the benefit of a population by now accustomed to the good things in life.

Almost all of what made Egypt and Alexandria great was put in place by the first two Ptolemies, Ptolemy I Soter and his equally capable son, Ptolemy II Philadelphus. The kingdom reached its apogee under Ptolemy III (every male ruler of Egypt was called Ptolemy, so most were identified by a further epithet such as Euergetes, by which Ptolemy III identified himself as 'the Benefactor'). In 242 BC Ptolemy Euergetes was in the process of kicking the stuffing out of the rival Greek Seleucid empire in the Middle East when he was forced to return home by a native uprising.

Ptolemy Euergetes knew that the secret to keeping the Egyptian people content with his rule was close cooperation with the priestly caste, so cooperation with the priests was enshrined in a declaration called the Canopus Decree. As was the Ptolemaic habit, this decree was published in three writing systems: hieroglyphs, to satisfy the conservative priestly caste; demotic, which was the script that contemporary Egyptians could actually read; and Greek, the language of Egypt's ruling caste. Later Egyptologists have been eternally grateful to the Ptolemies for this because it was a later decree, written on what is today called the Rosetta Stone, that proved the key to unlocking and understanding hieroglyphs and thus the early history of Egypt.

Egypt's downhill slide began under Ptolemy IV Philopater. The major event of his reign was a victory over the resurgent Seleucid kingdom at the Battle of Raphia in 217 BC (at around the same time that the Romans were experiencing the first of a series of defeats at the hands of Hannibal in a war which was seen at the time as only of significance to the antagonists). Ptolemy's victory was won by his phalanx [of pike-wielding heavy infantry], which for the first time included a levy of trained native Egyptians. On their return to Egypt, these phalangites demonstrated the value of their military experience by spearheading a nationalist revolt in southern Egypt, a revolt only suppressed after a long and costly war.

Ptolemy IV was scathingly criticized by contemporary historians for his love of luxury and his habit of leaving important decisions to senior advisors. This became a feature of life in the later Ptolemaic court, which combined this debilitating trait with the traditional brother-sister marriage (Ptolemy IV married his elder sister Arsinoe) and increasingly lethal dynastic infighting. Ptolemy IV's chief advisor, Sosimus, oversaw a purge of Ptolemy III's supporters when the next Ptolemy came to power. Ptolemy's brother, Magas, was painfully scalded to death in his bath, and Ptolemy's mother, who was generally believed to have favoured Magas, died so suddenly and unexpectedly that poison was widely suspected.

Then, in 204 BC, while the rebellion in southern Egypt was still raging, Ptolemy IV and his sister-wife died suddenly and suspiciously, leaving power in the hands of an advisor who placed himself in charge of the couple's five-year-old son and heir. The advisor was speedily disposed of, partly at the instigation of the Alexandrians who were becoming increasingly assertive about who ruled them and how.

When he came to maturity Ptolemy V Epiphanes himself proved unexpectedly competent, but the political paralysis during his youth had cost the country, both in drawing out the rebellion in the south and because Egypt's rivals took advantage of the country's weakness to strip away many overseas possessions.

Among these predatory foreign powers was Rome, now victorious over Carthage and confident enough to challenge – and defeat – the Hellenistic kingdoms of Macedon and the Seleucids. Egypt and the Seleucids had a long-standing rivalry (as demonstrated by over half a dozen major wars), and Egypt and Rome quickly formed an alliance based upon the principle that 'the enemy of my enemy is my friend' (a later Arab proverb). In this alliance the declining power of Egypt was always secondary to the rising power of Rome.

This was first demonstrated in the reign of Ptolemy V during the fifth of the wars with the Seleucids (202-195 BC). When the Seleucid king seemed about to invade Egypt, the Romans sent an emissary who flatly demanded that the Seleucid forces withdraw – which they did. However, at the end of that war, the Romans did not return to the Egyptians the overseas possessions the Romans had recaptured from Egypt's enemies. Instead, they kept these as their own to distribute to client kings and allies. At the same time Rome's growing population began to develop the dependence on Egyptian grain which was to continue for the next 500 years.

In the period after the (also sudden and suspicious) death of Ptolemy V, Egypt went into a period of prolonged decline. This had nothing to do with economic or social factors, and everything to do with the spiralling decadence of the Ptolemaic dynasty whose rivalries convulsed and impoverished the country over a century of intermittent civil war. The weakness and often the youth of the pharaohs (the Ptolemies had started dying young, and seldom from natural causes) allowed the rise of increasingly powerful, competing aristocratic factions. These factions often picked a Ptolemaic figurehead for their power struggles, and where there was a shortage of male Ptolemies to chose from, they sometimes selected a Cleopatra instead.

There had been Cleopatras around in Egypt almost as long as there had been Ptolemies. The first Queen Cleopatra was a wife of Philip II of Macedon and thus related by marriage to Philip's son, Alexander the Great. Alexander – the founder of Alexandria – also had a sister called Cleopatra who became queen of the neighbouring state of Epirus.

Interestingly, the connection with Egypt and dynastic infighting goes back even further, deep into the mists of Greek mythology. The very first of the Cleopatras was a Danaid, one of fifty legendary maidens forced to marry the fifty sons of an invader. The women did so, and all (but one) killed their husbands on their wedding night (a story immortalized in Aeschylus' play *The Supplicants*). The invader was a man called Aegyptus, after whom the country was named. So from the very beginning Cleopatras were associated with Egypt and with lethally dysfunctional marriages.

The first Egyptian Cleopatra of note was the queen of Ptolemy V. She took over control of Egypt after the sudden and convenient death of her husband and continued to rule the kingdom until her death some time around 177 BC. Her daughter, Cleopatra II, perfectly embodies the confusion of the later Ptolemaic dynasty. Cleopatra II kept a grip on the kingdom by sequentially marrying two of her brothers, Ptolemy VI and Ptolemy VIII, both of whom she also periodically went to war and feuded with. (The Ptolemy in between, Ptolemy VII, was killed by Ptolemy VIII before Cleopatra II had the chance to marry him.) Cleopatra II fell out with her husband Ptolemy VIII when he also married her daughter Cleopatra III, and after a brisk civil war Ptolemy VIII and Cleopatra III were driven out of Egypt. So incestuous were dynastic affairs at this point that Cleopatra III was married to her uncle with her mother as a co-wife, who was married to her own brother, which made Cleopatra III cousin to herself. Thereafter things really got confusing.

By the time of the death of Cleopatra III in 101 BC Egypt had moved briskly through to Ptolemy X (who had Cleopatra III murdered). This dynastic infighting and inbreeding left the Ptolemies little energy to do much of anything else, and the kingdom had by now basically conceded control of its foreign affairs to Rome. While Egypt sank into decline, Rome had grown ever more powerful and had conquered Macedon and mopped up the remnants of the Seleucid empire which had been falling apart with dynastic problems of its own.

Because Egypt was a major source of the Roman corn supply the Romans tried to keep track of Egypt's chaotic politics. (The modern numbering system of Ptolemies I-XVI is a modern convention, partly based upon guesswork. Ancient historians went by the epithets of the different Ptolemies and were as muddled as everyone else.) Rome also intervened whenever it was felt that an insufficiently compliant Ptolemy had risen to the top. Thus, for example, in 80 BC the Romans felt that the current ruler, Cleopatra Berenice, needed a more pro-Roman husband. Consequently, Cleopatra Berenice married her stepson, cousin and half-brother, all of which relatives were embodied in the single person of Ptolemy XI. As soon as he was married Ptolemy XI promptly and simultaneously committed matricide, sororicide and murder by killing Cleopatra Berenice.

At this point the Alexandrian people intervened. After the disastrous southern rebellion and several other flare-ups since, southern Egypt was mutinous but subdued. However, Alexandria, seat of the Ptolemaic kings, was mutinous and anything but subdued. The Alexandrians were at this time a polyglot mixture, the main ingredients of which were Greeks, Jews and native Egyptians. Neither the Greeks nor the Jews had much time for oppressive rulers, and the native Egyptians had long demonstrated their dislike of foreign rule.

Therefore, for a Ptolemaic ruler the secret to keeping a grip on Alexandria was carefully managing the different factions within the city and playing them off against each other. It helped a lot that the Greek and Jewish factions heartily disliked one other. It did not help at all that the later Ptolemies were hardly capable of balancing on a chair, let alone balancing the demands of Alexandria's volatile factions.

The Cleopatras seem to have been more capable administrators, and Cleopatra Berenice was actually rather popular in Alexandria at the time that she was murdered. This murder turned out to be a mistake, albeit one that Ptolemy XI did not have long to regret. The Alexandrians mobbed his guards and killed him just days into his sole rule.

Once Ptolemy XI had joined his slain spouse, Cleopatra Berenice, in the afterworld, the Egyptians looked around for a new ruler. Their choice needed to be acceptable to the aristocratic factions at court, to the people of the Egyptian interior, to the Alexandrians and, above all, to the Romans. The candidate eventually chosen to become Ptolemy XII of Egypt was a son of Ptolemy IX who is commonly known as 'Auletes' (the flute-player) because of his fondness for playing that instrument.

One of Auletes' strengths was that he was not conceived in a brother-sister marriage but as the result of a liaison by Ptolemy IX with another woman. Exactly which woman is a matter of considerable dispute, and a matter which was probably of considerable interest to Julius Caesar, since Auletes was the father of that Cleopatra (VII) who was his ally and paramour while he was in Alexandria.

Auletes the pharaoh was very much a Roman puppet, though history prefers to give him the somewhat more flattering name of 'client king'. Auletes spent his youth outside Egypt, mostly for his own protection. Indeed, he was abroad when the Egyptians summoned him home to take the throne, whereupon the new pharaoh immediately demonstrated that he was a true Ptolemy by marrying his sister, Cleopatra V. Nevertheless, Auletes' dubious legitimacy put him on a weak footing with regard to the Romans, because a previous Ptolemy (Ptolemy X) had left Egypt to Rome in his will. This transfer of ownership was only valid if the pharaoh had left no legitimate heirs, and many Romans argued that Ptolemy X was indeed the last legitimate king of Egypt.

Auletes recognized that those Romans wanting to annex Egypt were largely driven by greed, so his solution was to assuage that greed by paying Roman politicians a huge sum of money without their having to go to the bother of taking his country to get it. Among the beneficiaries of these large cash contributions were both Julius Caesar and Pompey, who were at this time (59 BC) allies and dominant in Roman politics. The need for the huge bribes paid to keep Egypt even nominally independent became clear when the Romans decided quite arbitrarily to annex Cyprus in 58 BC.

Cyprus had until then been an Egyptian possession, so this annexation added to the sense of anger and impotence felt by the Egyptians, who were already seething under the burden of massively increased taxes which were funnelled directly into Roman pockets without benefiting the country at all. The subsequent civil unrest, especially in Alexandria, increased to the point where Auletes was forced to flee from Egypt before he was lynched as his predecessor had been. The Egyptians chose his daughter Berenice as their new ruler and insisted that she adopt a more independent stance.

Naturally Auletes turned to the Romans for assistance and just as naturally the Romans agreed – in return for the promise of yet further large sums of money to be transferred to those Romans responsible for securing that agreement. Chief among Auletes' backers in the Senate was Pompey, who lent his support less for the money (he was already fantastically wealthy) than because he had established close ties with Auletes while campaigning in the East.

Aulus Gabinius, the Roman who was to lead the force that restored Auletes to power, allegedly received a payment of 10,000 talents (approximately 300,000,000 US dollars) for doing so. Thus, in 55 BC, backed with the force of Roman swords, Auletes retook his throne. The usurper Berenice paid for her youthful rebellion with her life (she was twenty-two years old) and Auletes resumed his role as a conduit between the Egyptian taxpayers and their Roman beneficiaries.

Yet by now Auletes was ailing. He made his daughter Cleopatra VII his co-regent and simplified the process of handing his country's money to the Romans by making a Roman called Rabirius his minister of finance. Rabirius did his job so enthusiastically that the indignant Egyptians chased him out of Egypt and he was later tried for extortion in Rome.

In 51 BC Auletes died, leaving his kingdom to his daughter Cleopatra VII (henceforth for simplicity simply called Cleopatra) and his son Ptolemy XIII (with yet more Ptolemies to come, the numerical suffix must remain). Again Pompey was instrumental in making sure that the Roman Senate endorsed the succession of the new joint monarchy.

Cleopatra was a powerful personality and she immediately began to take the country in hand. There were several major issues confronting her. Firstly, of course, her country was massively in debt to Rome. Secondly, the Roman legionary force which had re-installed her father in power had remained in the country as a de facto garrison. Probably because they had been unpaid for some time, these soldiers were becoming increasingly predatory and mutinous. Finally, the flooding of the Nile had been lower than usual, with consequent poor harvests to compound Egypt's problems.

As Cleopatra leaned into fixing these issues. Ptolemy XIII became increasingly sidelined and resentful. This mattered less then the fact that Cleopatra had also alienated the court faction aligned with her brother. This group of powerful aristocrats backing Ptolemy XIII channelled popular resentment at Egypt's straitened circumstances against the queen. Usually at this point one or both of the squabbling groups of Egyptian courtiers would have sent a delegation appealing to the Romans for support. However, by now Rome was fully preoccupied with its own civil war. Julius Caesar had just crossed the Rubicon and was in the process of taking over Italy.

As a loyal client, Cleopatra duly sent military support to her patron Pompey in the form of sixty warships. Rather adroitly she also gave Pompey a contingent of her troublesome garrison of Roman mercenary soldiers, thus simultaneously getting rid of one of Egypt's problems while repaying her debts. Sadly, a preoccupied Pompey was unable to reciprocate with support for Cleopatra against Ptolemy XIII. Nor was Cleopatra able to get rid of one of her major headaches – the remaining legionaries left by Gabinius as a garrison to hold down the country. These men known as 'the Gabinians' were a powerful force mostly loyal to themselves and their privileges. They currently supported the faction of Ptolemy XIII because they saw this as the winning side.

Outclassed militarily, Cleopatra and her younger sister Arsinoe were driven out of Egypt and forced to take refuge in the Roman province of Syria. Once there, the undeterred Cleopatra set about raising a mercenary army of her own. She was in the process of fighting her way back into Egypt to unseat Ptolemy XIII when the battle which was to change the course of her life took place at Pharsalus between Pompey and Caesar.

Being Cleopatra, the young woman did not wait to see how this seismic change in Roman affairs was going to affect the outcome of her personal civil war. Instead, she pushed on with her army across the Sinai, determined that, should Caesar's victory at Pharsalus prove decisive, when the new master of the Roman world turned his attention towards Egypt he would find Cleopatra enthroned in Alexandria.

Chapter 3

The Road to Alexandria – Caius Julius Caesar

If Pompey was somewhat strange in being a general who was not very good at fighting battles, Julius Caesar was even more of an anomaly. He was a politician who was so good at getting people to hate him that it was practically a superpower. One major reason for the civil war which broke out in 49 BC was because the bitter, visceral hatred of influential Roman aristocrats for Caesar blinded them to reason. Under pressure from those aristocrats, not only did the Senate refuse to negotiate, it also abandoned legality by ignoring a tribunican veto of its actions.

There was something about Caesar that rubbed people up the wrong way, especially those people in positions of power. These men were the lords of Rome at a time when Rome dominated the known world. Caesar should have been one of them. His family was ancient nobility – in fact Caesar traced his ancestry back past the foundation of Rome to long-lost Troy and the goddess Venus. While the Caesars had been eclipsed in previous generations by the rise of more powerful clans, by the time of Caesar's birth the family was rising again to prominence. All that Caesar had to do was toe the line of accepted aristocratic behaviour and his family connections and their political clout almost guaranteed him a seat in the Senate, high office and important military commands.

While Caesar was not quite one of those high aristocrats whom Cicero bitterly described as being 'made consuls in their cradles', Caesar was close. Had he followed the conventional Roman route to power by cultivating influential senators, wheeling and dealing in favours, bribes and back-room deals and standing for the appropriate magisterial offices at appropriate times, Caesar would have gone far. He would have made the necessary friends, followed by a strategic marriage and a timely divorce and remarriage or two, and on the strength of his superb oratory and the political clout of his clan he could have become a praetor, a consul and even censor without unduly ruffling any senatorial feathers.

Yet things did not work out that way. One of Caesar's problems was that he was one of the most brilliant men of his generation – but his brilliance did not extend to knowing when to shut up about it. Caesar saw himself as not just the equal of the greatest men in Rome but their superior, and he was not shy about advertising that fact. Plutarch at the start of his *Life of Caesar* points out that the young Caesar began his political career by going out of his way to antagonize the murderous Sulla just when he was in the process of killing off by the hundred the allies of his arch-enemy Marius.

Plutarch says 'Caesar was not prepared to be overlooked by Sulla, and so put himself before the electorate as candidate for a priesthood'. (Many top religious positions in Rome had elected priests.) This got Sulla's attention, especially as Caesar was related by marriage to Sulla's arch-enemy Marius, whom Sulla had just defeated in a vicious civil war. He goes on:

> Sulla was planning to have Caesar executed, and when others said there was no reason to kill a mere boy, Sulla declared that they were idiots if they could not see in that "boy" many Mariuses.'
> (Plutarch, *Caesar* 1.3)

Caesar's powerful family connections saved his life on that occasion, but his talent for losing friends and alienating people continued to create headwinds in a life which should have been smooth sailing. For a start, rather than be embarrassed by his close family ties with the populist Marius, Caesar heartily embraced the connection. This made him popular with the voters who remembered Marius fondly, but hardly endeared Caesar to the Senate which was profoundly anti-Marius, not least because Sulla had recently killed off any senator who wasn't.

This set the pattern for Caesar's career – cocking a snoot at the Senate while going out of his way to ingratiate himself with the people at every opportunity.

> It is believed that Cicero was the first to see what underlay Caesar's conduct and to fear it as one might fear the dangers beneath the smiling surface of the sea. Cicero understood the power of the character who hid beneath that generous and cheerful exterior and wondered if his political ambitions were set on establishing a tyranny.
>
> 'And then', said Cicero 'I see his hair arranged with such immaculate precision, and watch him scratching his head with one finger [which the Romans believed to be a sign of a pathic sodomite] and it appears inconceivable that such a man might even think of overthrowing the Roman state.'
>
> (Plutarch, *Caesar* 4)

Rome, in however flawed a fashion, was a democracy and that meant that Caesar was capable of rising to high office whether his political opponents (ie almost everybody in the Roman establishment) liked it or not. For example, there was the office of *pontifex maximus*, a priestly office so important that in later years the title was claimed by the Pope – and which the Pope has held ever since. By Roman convention this priesthood was held by a senior politician as a sort of reward for long service to the state. In this case, the politician whom the Roman establishment reckoned was due the post was Metellus Pius, of Rome's distinguished family of the Caecilii Metelli.

Instead, the upstart Caesar took a huge risk and stood against Metellus, confident that his popularity with the people would carry him through. It did, and also earned Caesar the undying enmity of the Metelli, members of which clan were later among the foremost in pressing to have Caesar removed from office at all costs, even if this meant civil war.

Caesar was popular with the people because he spent extravagantly on public benefactions and because his demagogic approach was popular with those who – rightly – suspected the Senate of being packed with members far more interested in private gain than the public good. From Caesar's perspective the problem with buying popular support was that he was spending money that he did not have, and the size of his debts was colossal. Fortunately one of his few supporters was Licinius Crassus, a cynical political operator who saw in the amoral Caesar the perfect cats-paw to push his own behind-the-scenes agenda.

Crassus bailed Caesar out of some early financial pickles, and in later years Caesar was able to pay his own way thanks to successful military commands. Whatever his limitations as a politician, no-one could doubt Caesar's abilities as a general – especially as in his books Caesar himself has carefully explained to his contemporaries and to posterity exactly how brilliant he was. Caesar's first major command was in Spain, where he paid off his debts and made a small fortune by attacking and looting the towns of Rome's enemies. It was true – as Caesar's enemies pointed out – that many of these unfortunate contributors to Caesar's bank account had not been Rome's enemies until Caesar attacked them, but Roman perfidy in Spain was by then a long and dishonourable tradition and certainly Caesar was not alone in acting this way.

When Crassus needed legal help to assist some of his political allies, he decided that Caesar would be ideal for the job of passing the appropriate laws. Therefore, he was prepared to back Caesar for the consulship despite the violent objections of most of the Roman

Senate (which had just outmanoeuvred Caesar in his attempt to claim a triumph for his efforts in Spain). However, so entrenched was opposition to Caesar that further heavyweight support was needed, and this was found in the person whom Caesar was later to face at Pharsalus – Gnaeus Pompey.

Pompey had returned to Rome after a successful campaign in Asia Minor and the Levant to find the Senate deeply suspicious of his wealth and popularity. As a result, when Pompey sought land for his disbanded soldiers, the Senate resisted. (Senators were always averse to changes in land legislation in case it affected their own property, much of which they had acquired in legally dubious ways.) While Pompey and Crassus were far from friends, they buried their differences in the cause of mutual serviceability. Or, as the Romans put it, *'manus manum lavat'*, one hand washes the other. To further consolidate the partnership, Caesar married his daughter to Pompey, thus becoming his later adversary's father-in-law.

Though the junior partner in the triumvirate, Caesar was quick to use it for his own benefit and secured himself command of the Roman provinces of Gaul. This was over the vehement opposition of many senators who wanted to award Caesar the less-sparkling potential command of Supervisor of Italy's Fields and Forests. Once he had provincial command, Caesar used the pretext of protecting Gaul from an invasion of Germanic tribes to basically take over the entire country. The Gauls did not submit quietly and rose in a nationalist rebellion which was only suppressed with difficulty.

Caesar's problem was that while gaining power and wealth in Gaul (and killing and enslaving over a million of its inhabitants to further his political ambitions) he was necessarily outside Rome, and therefore his political influence in the capital was limited. This was not a problem while he had Crassus and Pompey to guard his back, but Crassus died while campaigning (disastrously) against the Parthians, and Pompey became more distant once Caesar's daughter had died after giving birth to his child.

As a result, Caesar had the tricky problem of how to extricate himself from Gaul without leaving himself open to the malice of his many enemies in the Roman Senate. It certainly did not help that Pompey had gone from being an ally to becoming instead a close associate of the anti-Caesar faction. It was at this point that Caesar's long career of alienating potential allies came back to bite him. The only supporters he had in the Senate were those whom he had been able to buy with his now very considerable wealth. As Caesar's biographer Suetonius puts it:

> Caesar was the comfort and abettor of all [aristocrats] who had legal problems or where in debt. He would help any young spendthrift unless their talent for loose living had left them so mired in guilt or poverty that there was no saving them. These people Caesar plainly informed that their only hope lay in a civil war.
>
> (Suetonius, *Caesar* 27)

Useful as such supporters were, they were not an adequate counterweight to the very many important Roman aristocrats who loathed the very ground that Caesar walked upon.

Yet Caesar could not stay in Gaul forever. His extended period of command had come to an end and his return to Rome was inevitable. The question that he had to consider – and a question to which the rest of the Roman world was anxiously awaiting an answer – was whether he should come alone or with his army. Caesar was well aware that, should he enter Italy as a private citizen, then his massed enemies would be waiting to haul him to court on charges which basically amounted to the horrendous crime of being Julius Caesar. Whatever the crime listed on the actual docket, Caesar was in little doubt that he would be found guilty of it. Thereafter he faced bankruptcy and exile at best and execution at worst.

Caesar lobbied hard to be allowed to keep his command until he could stand for a second consulship, since if he could enter Italy as a consul he would be immune from prosecution. Then, as head of the Roman Republic, he could use his year in office to mollify, bribe or otherwise defuse the enemy coalition aligned against him.

At this point there were three major players in the high-stakes political game. There was Caesar and his allies – mostly men indebted to him such as the tribune Mark Antony; there was the anti-Caesar faction in the Roman Senate; and there was Pompey. Nervously watching were the majority of senators and the common people, with both sets of observers uneasily aware that Rome's republic trembled on the brink of dissolution. It should be added that the risk to the Republic was every bit as much due to the corruption and misgovernment of the current regime as it was to Caesar's relentless accumulation of personal power.

Caesar tried hard to find a way out of the impasse, but Pompey's ever-growing closeness to Caesar's enemies emboldened them to refuse any attempt at compromise. In the end Caesar had to accept that as a politician he had failed. All that he could now do was attempt to be better than Pompey at being a general. Accordingly in the fateful year of 49 BC Caesar set out for Rome, bringing with him his veteran legions. As soon as those legions moved out of Caesar's province, which they did on 10 January by crossing the little River Rubicon which marked the southern boundary of Cisalpine Gaul, Caesar ceased to be a Roman proconsul and became a rebel in arms against the Roman state.

It says something about Caesar's enemies that this somehow caught them flat-footed, even though they had been striving for months to effect this very outcome. As we have seen, Pompey was unable to deliver the support which he had assumed was his thanks to the prestige of his reputation. ('If I stamp my foot, Italy will rise', he had boasted. He stamped, and it didn't.) Consequently Pompey was forced to make a precipitous retreat from Italy to regroup in Greece. Caesar did not immediately follow his enemies eastward but instead concentrated on securing his rear by consolidating his grip on Italy and conquering Spain.

Then with Gaul, Italy and Spain – somewhat precariously – in his grasp, Caesar finally crossed to Greece for the decisive campaign of the civil wars. Again as we have seen, his struggle with Pompey in Greece almost ended in disaster. Pompey's skill at large-scale manoeuvre and logistics brought Caesar to the brink of defeat before Caesar's enemies did him the huge favour of doing what Caesar himself could not – they made Pompey stand and gamble everything on a pitched battle. After the carnage, Caesar viewed the field strewn with the corpses of Roman soldiers and senators and exclaimed in sorrow and frustration, 'this is what they wanted!'

While the defeat of the army of the Republic at Pharsalus was a major victory, Caesar was well aware that his victory would not be decisive until he had captured the commander of that army – Pompey himself. The person of Pompey was one of the great prizes of the war because, given time, Pompey was quite capable of raising a new army and it was quite certain that he would not give Caesar another opportunity to defeat that army in battle.

Already there were other armies being raised by Caesar's enemies. Cato Uticensis was putting together a handy force in the province of Africa, and Pompey's sons were about to do the same in Spain. Yet Caesar did not fear Republican armies without Pompey or Pompey without an army. It was the combination of both that he had to avoid at all costs. It was for this reason that Caesar had failed to anticipate Pompey's flight eastwards after Pharsalus. Had Caesar been Pompey he would have headed directly for the nearest troops to replace those he had lost in the recent battle, and these were in Macedonia (which always had a substantial garrison to repel barbarian tribes attacking from the north).

Once Caesar had determined Pompey's direction of flight he immediately set out in pursuit. However, even Caesar's famous *celeritas* – his talent for speedy manoeuvre – was hampered by the fact that he was now personally in charge of much of the Roman world. Some parts of that world, such as the part he had just conquered after Pharsalus, were in considerable disarray, and if Caesar did not want anarchy or counter-revolution breaking out behind him then some time and effort had to be diverted from chasing Pompey and dedicated to setting matters in order.

A quick way of doing this was to grant autonomy to captured areas. Thus Caesar speedily got out of Thessaly where he had been fighting by giving the region its 'freedom'. This meant that the cities of Thessaly were relieved of Roman taxation and allowed to run their own affairs. This saved Caesar the time he did not have to spend sorting out matters in the area, and simultaneously guaranteed that the Thessalians would fight ferociously on his behalf to retain their newfound privileges.

In Asia Minor, Caesar found Rome's possessions in financial disarray because Pompey and his supporters had ruthlessly looted the region to pay for their war. Caesar applied a quick fix by way of a judicious tax cut and then once again launched himself in pursuit of Pompey whom he had now determined to be en route to Alexandria. Pompey had decided upon Egypt as his new base because of the many advantages it offered him, and being an equally competent strategist, Caesar immediately saw the threat that Pompey's move presented. 'He feared that Pompey, by occupying that country, might again become strong', remarks Cassius Dio (*History* 42.7).

It now became imperative that Caesar stop Pompey before his rival gained control of Egypt. After all, Egypt's major issues were poor governance and indebtedness to Rome. Under Pompey Egypt would be well-governed and certainly not paying anything to Caesar's Rome. The state had powerful armies already mobilized because of the developing civil war between Cleopatra and Ptolemy XIII. Should these armies be unified under Pompey's command then Caesar had a real problem, because Egypt was highly defensible. Caesar could not attack by sea, because he lacked a fleet, and (as Alexander the Great had discovered a few centuries before) fighting in through Gaza took a long time – and with the rest of Rome's empire in danger of slipping from his grasp, time was something that Caesar did not have.

Even if guaranteed success – which was in fact by no means certain – Caesar could not afford to give Pompey the months it would take for Caesar to gather his forces and launch a conventional invasion of Egypt. By the time Caesar had finally conquered Egypt he might have lost the rest of the empire. This took option A – a properly organized invasion – off the table. Therefore Caesar' was left with option B – to follow on Pompey's heels as closely as possible with whatever forces he had with him at that moment and hope to wrest Egypt from Pompey's grasp before his rival was able to seize control of the country.

This was something of a gamble, because the forces Caesar had on hand were distinctly unimpressive. He had just two legions under his command, even though one of these legions was the Sixth. Legio VI had an impressive record. Caesar himself had raised the legion in Cisalpine Gaul (thus further infuriating the Senate, which believed it was in charge of recruiting Roman legionaries) and the legion's soldiers had fought in some of the toughest campaigns of the Gallic war, including the battle at Cenabum (modern Orleans) and the defeat of Vercingetorix at Alesia.

In 49 BC the legion was fighting to secure Spain for Caesar in the civil war. It then transferred to Greece to help win the battle of Pharsalus. If Caesar's recruiters had offered the young men of Cisalpine Gaul the chance to join the army and see the world, Caesar was certainly delivering on that promise. The problem was that members of the Sixth had also been dying all over the world, and the casualties had not been replaced.

> The Sixth Legion … had endured such trials and dangers and difficulties in marches and voyages that the stress of campaigning had severely reduced it in size.
>
> (*The Alexandrine War* 76)

Normally a legion would contain 6,000 men. At this point the Sixth was less than half that size – and it was about to get a lot smaller. But at least the Sixth contained loyal veteran soldiers who made up in ferocity and skill what they lacked in numbers. The same could not be said for Caesar's other legion, Legio XXVIII. Caesar had taken over the Twenty-eighth soon after Pharsalus, and the legion contained mainly raw, unskilled levies. Since the men had been recruited by Pompey the loyalty of the troops was also questionable. Nor did the legion make up in numbers what it lacked in every other way, for it contained just 2,200 men. This gave Caesar at most 5-6,000 men with whom to force his will upon an entire country, a country already in arms and which contained not one but two armies each larger than his own.

Undeterred Caesar hastily packed his men into transports, which were escorted by a squadron of ten warships from the friendly island of Rhodes. Rather as Caesar's Sixth Legion were few but ferocious fighters, the Rhodians could supply few ships but they were perhaps the best sailors in the world at the time. If Caesar met with a hostile Roman fleet he was doomed, but the Rhodians would at least protect his transports from smaller enemy elements and the pirates who had taken advantage of the chaos of war to resume the trade which Pompey had recently and successfully suppressed. Caesar himself describes his forces as follows:

> Caesar took with him to Alexandria one legion under his command from Thessaly [ie Legio VI] and another which he had summoned from the province of Achaea [Legio XXVIII] … he had also 800 cavalry [German mercenaries] and ten warships from Rhodes and a few others from [the province of] Asia. There were around 3,200 men in the legions … but Caesar did not hesitate to advance even with this weak support. He trusted that his reputation would make any place safe for him.
>
> (Caesar, *Civil Wars* 106)

As he left Asia Minor, Caesar may have reflected that he had expected a final showdown with Pompey in Italy after he had crossed the Rubicon. Then he had crossed to Greece expecting that he would there have to settle things with Pompey once and for all. Now he was leaving Asia Minor for Alexandria, and once again expecting that this time he and Pompey would finally resolve their long-standing rivalry. All roads it seemed, led to Alexandria.

Chapter 4

Murder on the Nile

Like Caesar, Pompey had crossed to Egypt with a somewhat rag-tag fleet. He himself was aboard a full-fledged warship which he had obtained in Cyprus and others of his followers had also managed to take possession of enough ships to give him a decent escort. Those who had not been able to obtain military vessels by bribes, favours or threats tagged along in commandeered or rented merchant ships.

The little fleet's destination was not Alexandria, the capital of Egypt, but the relatively minor port of Per-Amun which the Romans called Pelusium. Like Alexandria, Pelusium was on the Nile Delta but, since the delta was some 250km across where it met the Mediterranean, this still put some distance between the port and Alexandria itself. The significant thing about Pelusium was not the silt-choked harbour, but the fact that it stood on the only solid ground between salt marshes to the south and the sea to the north.

This made Pelusium a significant choke point for traffic entering Egypt by way of Gaza, and the Ptolemies had gone to considerable lengths to make that traffic more difficult should they wish to do so. By the time of Pompey's arrival this gateway to Egypt from the northeast was a substantial border fortress, for all that a decade ago it had put up little resistance when the Romans had come from Syria to restore Ptolemy XII Auletes to his throne. (The leader of the Roman force that took Pelusium on that occasion was a dashing young cavalry commander called Mark Antony.)

Now Ptolemy XIII, the son of Ptolemy Auletes, was at Pelusium, determined that on this occasion the city would keep out invaders from the northeast, although in this case the invader was his sister-wife Cleopatra. Just to add a further dash of complication to the teenage pharaoh's already somewhat complex existence, it was around this time that another of his sisters also declared against him. This new enemy was his sister Arsinoe and it is uncertain if she was at this time an ally of Cleopatra or already a rival. Nevertheless, it seems clear that even if she had not yet declared her intentions to Cleopatra, the ambitious Arsinoe saw herself as coming to the Egyptian throne over the corpses of her squabbling siblings.

Just when it seemed that things could not get any more complex, messengers reached the court of the beleaguered Ptolemy XIII informing him that Gnaeus Pompey of Rome had arrived and wanted a word with the pharaoh about involving Egypt in the war which had engulfed the rest of the Mediterranean world. This was a lot to unload upon a youth who was of an age where his biggest concern should have been how to cope with a first wave of acne, so unsurprisingly Ptolemy turned to his advisors.

It has already been mentioned that the later Ptolemies tended to come to the throne young and remain briefly. This was because older pharaohs (such as the relatively long-lived Ptolemy Auletes) tended to develop personalities of their own which made them less amenable to those people who fancied themselves as the true rulers of Egypt – the rival factions who stood behind each family member and used them as figureheads to support their own interests. It was precisely because the strong-willed Cleopatra had refused to be used as a puppet in this way that her enemies had united behind Ptolemy XIII to force her from Egypt.

Chief among Cleopatra's enemies was a eunuch called Pothinus. Because Ptolemy XIII had become pharaoh at the tender age of eleven years old, Pothinus had been selected to serve as regent until the lad came of age. Two other courtiers served as guardians to the young king, namely a general called Achillas and an orator called Theodotus of Chios. These men had been dismayed when Ptolemy

Auletes died and his will revealed that the late king had wanted not only Ptolemy XIII to take the throne, but also his sister Cleopatra. (It is often speculated that Ptolemy Auletes also specified in his will that the royal pair should marry, but this is not certain.)

If the three men behind Ptolemy XIII were upset by the accession of Cleopatra as co-ruler, they were outraged when Cleopatra began to rule as if her brother – and by extension themselves – did not matter. From the perspective of the triumvirate who guided the young Ptolemy XIII it was only reasonable that if Cleopatra stood in the way of their indirect rule of Egypt then Cleopatra would have to go. True, removing Cleopatra from the scene was proving somewhat more difficult than expected, but the ambitious threesome had every expectation that they could keep Egypt's stubborn queen at bay at Pelusium.

Pompey was a different matter. Whatever their moral deficiencies, the three men behind the throne of Ptolemy XIII were certainly not politically naive. When Pompey's ambassadors announced his arrival in Egypt it was immediately clear to them that Pompey had not come as a refugee or a supplicant (though he would have been a major problem even if he had merely done that). Instead, Pompey had come to turn Egypt into the centre of Rome's resistance to the military coup of Julius Caesar. Should that happen the three men would again be sidelined, and this time by a Roman with whom they would have little chance of gaining influence.

Pothinus called a conference of the young Pharaoh's advisors to work out their next steps. Various options were debated and rejected before the orator Theodotus took the floor. There was only one way out of the crisis, Theodotus informed his listeners. Pompey must be killed. If they drove Pompey from their shores and his cause ultimately prevailed, then Egypt would face severe punishment for rejecting Pompey in his hour of need. On the other hand, Theodotus pointed out, 'If we take him in, we will have Caesar as an enemy and Pompey for a master.' (Plutarch, *Pompey* 77.4)

Given the lethal nature of Egyptian politics, no-one seriously considered that Caesar would receive the news of Pompey's death with anything other than joyful relief. After all, leading Egyptians had been slaying close family members for generations and the people currently leading the pharaoh's army were working very hard to accomplish the death of the pharaoh's sisters. Given this perspective, no-one could imagine that Caesar would feel much grief about the death of a former son-in-law. Accordingly, once Theodotus had provided the logic, the execution (literally) of the plan was put in the hands of Achillas, the military man of the threesome.

Achillas was determined that Pompey should not meet with Ptolemy XIII, or indeed actually set foot on Egyptian soil. His fear was that the young pharaoh might be so dazzled by Pompey that he would agree to allow his country to become the base of Roman resistance to Caesar. Furthermore, the Gabinian legionaries were still nominally Roman soldiers and a good number had actually served under Pompey in the past. So if Pompey did gain a foothold in Egypt, the Gabinians would provide him with an instant garrison with which to enforce his will. Therefore, Pompey must be lured off his ship and killed before he disembarked in Egypt.

Reasoning that Pompey would feel most at ease with fellow Romans, Achillas hastened to provide some. After a quick search through the ranks of the Gabinians, Achillas was delighted to find a veteran called Septimus who had actually served as a military tribune under Pompey, and also a former centurion of Pompey's called Salvius. These men were easily suborned towards treachery, presumably by the allocation of large sums of money. These Roman traitors Achillas took with him aboard a fishing boat and sailed out to meet Pompey's trireme.

Those aboard the trireme viewed the arrivals with deep suspicion. A few men on a fishing boat was hardly the royal reception they had been hoping for. Furthermore, more-powerful Egyptian navy vessels were already closing off Pompey's escape route, boarding his other ships and taking off the occupants. Pompey knew that things were not looking good, but at this point turning to flee would show that Pompey had decided that the Egyptians were hostile and this might provoke the very enmity that he feared.

Furthermore, one of his old soldiers was aboard the fishing boat greeting him as 'General', while Achillas apologized for the disrespectful greeting in a shabby boat. This boat, he explained, was necessary because the port of Pelusium had a sand-choked harbour (as indeed it did) and Pompey's trireme would run aground on the sandbanks around the fortress if it attempted to dock. Accordingly, and despite his reservations, Pompey climbed aboard the boat.

Plutarch describes how Pompey's wife Cornelia watched from the trireme as her husband sailed away. Pompey attempted to make conversation with the others on the boat but was met with grim silence. After a while he gave up the attempt and pulled out a small scroll on which he had written the speech with which he intended to address Ptolemy when they met. The ship reached the shore, and Pompey stood up to disembark. That was the signal for his treacherous ex-tribune to literally stab him in the back, with Achillas and Salvius the centurion joining in once Pompey was down.

Pompey's last act was to pull up the fold of his toga, thus covering his head as a pious Roman should when coming into the presence of the gods. (It might have given his ghost some satisfaction to know that in later years exactly the same gesture would be made for exactly the same reason as Julius Caesar died at the feet of his assassins.) Pompey's murderers stripped the body and tipped it overboard, but not before they had sawed off the head for later presentation to Caesar.

> So died Pompey, who with his death proved once again the fragility of human good fortune. Pompey was not incapable of foresight and had generally made himself secure against any potential vulnerabilities. Since he was a boy, by land and sea he had won victories in Asia and Europe, and unexpected victories in Africa – yet now in his fifty-eighth year he was unexpectedly

defeated for no very good reason. The master of the entire Roman sea [ie the Mediterranean] and of a thousand ships, nevertheless perished on that sea in a tiny boat. ...

In a sense, the man who had him killed was Ptolemy, that man to whose father Pompey had restored his land and his kingdom. It was that Ptolemy whom Roman soldiers were still guarding – Roman soldiers left behind by Gabinius. This had been done as a favour from Pompey who knew how the Egyptians had hated the young king's father – that same young king [whose advisors] had now put him to death.

(Cassius Dio, *History* 42.5)

Those on the trireme witnessed the murder and promptly proved that Pompey's worries about being unable to flee for safety were unfounded. With the help of a shore breeze Pompey's wife and retainers reached the safety of the open sea ahead of the pursuing Egyptians. This was little consolation to Pompey's distraught wife and Pompey's entourage. Not only had Cornelia lost a husband, but the cause for which Pompey had fought had taken a major and probably fatal blow. Without Pompey, Caesar's ultimate victory had gone from very probable to almost certain. All that Caesar needed to do was the mopping up.

For Pompey's remains a certain afterlife continued. One of the slaves who had been manning the boat decided to give Pompey a proper funeral – either out of respect for the dead, or perhaps because he was well aware that there might be unpleasant consequences for all involved in the killing of one of Rome's greatest sons. Accordingly, he wrapped the body properly and, with the help of another – more loyal – former soldier of Pompey's, he gave it as good a cremation as he could. Much later the ashes were restored to Pompey's widow who interred them with due ceremony at Pompey's farm in the Alban hills outside Rome.

None of this was known to Caesar who came rushing into Alexandria three days later. Caesar arrived with a slightly stronger force than he had expected due to one of those strokes of luck which regularly marked his career. En route to Egypt his little force had pulled into harbour at one of the many islands that dot the southeast Mediterranean. On arrival they discovered that a flotilla of Roman ships was already anchored there.

The commander of the flotilla was a supporter of Pompey and had just got word of the defeat at Pharsalus. He decided that Caesar had now come for him personally and so promptly surrendered, throwing himself at Caesar's mercy and placing his ships at Caesar's disposal. Caesar was grateful for the ships but may later have briefly regretted showing mercy. The man he spared – Gaius Cassius – was later one of the leaders of those who assassinated him on the Ides of March.

Once Caesar had arrived in Alexandria, he found that he could not leave. The etesian winds had set in from the north, pinning his ships inside the harbour. Fortunately, Caesar had already quite a few of his 5,000 men with him and he was eager to assure the Egyptians that more were on the way. This eagerness was partly prompted by the fact that Caesar had just discovered that the Egyptians had no compunction about killing high-ranking Romans. They had demonstrated this by presenting Caesar with Pompey's seal ring (a lion on a sword) and then, to demonstrate unequivocally that Pompey was dead, also with the head of the deceased.

Caesar recoiled from the latter with horror which may or may not have been feigned. On the one hand Pompey was a rival, a dangerous enemy and the main pillar of the resistance to his takeover of the empire. On the other hand, Pompey had once been a friend, a political ally and Caesar's son-in-law. To see so great a man reduced to a grisly souvenir might have given Caesar a few worrisome thoughts as to his own mortality. In any case, Caesar had public opinion in Rome to consider. Now that Pompey and the Senate had been replaced by Caesar the dictator, there were many in Italy who were wondering if they were on the right side. Reports of Caesar gloating over the head of the dead Pompey would not play well with such an audience.

(As an example of this a century later, we can see the propaganda made by his enemies when the Emperor Vitellius visited the battlefield which had secured his victory in the civil wars of AD 69. When his hosts apologized for the smell of the still-unburied corpses Vitellius genially replied, 'A dead enemy always smells good'. The emperor's opponents immediately played up this disrespect for the Roman dead, and Vitellius only lasted a few months longer. Whatever his true feelings, Caesar, who was working hard to show his magnanimity in victory, could hardly be expected to show joy at Pompey's demise, especially given the circumstances in which this demise had occurred.)

Nevertheless, while the rest of Caesar's transports were catching up with their high-speed general Caesar happily played tourist in Alexandria, acting as though Pompey's demise had removed his reason for being there and he was merely passing the time until he could sail off again. Once a good contingent of his little army had arrived and was properly organized, Caesar took a different tack. Suddenly he became a consul of Rome on a state visit to a client kingdom, a kingdom where affairs were to be organized as the Roman saw fit.

Even with his troops with him, Caesar was taking something of a gamble with this high-handed attitude. Annoyed by the Roman presence, the Alexandrians were already highly restive and had taken grave offence at Caesar advancing through their city preceded by lictors bearing the consular fasces. The citizens demonstrated their displeasure by minor riots and disturbances in which Caesar lost a few soldiers to the mob. Also, of course, things could still get much worse. Egypt had not one but two armies mobilized, either of which vastly outnumbered his little force.

In public Caesar acted as if none of this should be any concern of his, while in private he sent messages to his forces across the Mediterranean and nearby allies that they should head for Alexandria as fast as they could. Haughtily, Caesar announced to the Ptolemaic court that while he was in Egypt he would decide what to do about Egypt's massive debts. By one account Caesar took immediate steps to reduce that debt by ordering the imposition of large tax levies – something that caused widespread anger. This anger was tinged with outrage because Caesar ordered that the levy be also paid by the temples, and the Egyptians were 'the most religious people on Earth' (Dio 42.34).

Still acting as though he were the de facto ruler of Egypt, Caesar declared that he would personally arbitrate in the war between Cleopatra and Ptolemy XIII (and Arsinoe) and that while he was arbitrating both sides should immediately disband their armies.

Caesar's immediate problem was how to deal with the triumvirate of Ptolemy's advisors. These men were only slightly less happy to see Caesar than they had been to see Pompey. Their surly attitude made it plain that they wanted nothing more of Caesar than to see him sail off again and leave the Egyptians to their own affairs. As de facto host to Caesar, Pothinus made his position clear by providing Caesar's legionaries with barely edible rations. In a royal palace bulging with gold and silverware, his servants gave Caesar his meals on clay platters and wooden bowls, claiming that because of Egypt's debts the Romans had long ago taken everything more valuable. Meanwhile Pothinus and Achillas plotted furiously to get rid of the Roman interloper as expeditiously as possible.

When Caesar summoned Ptolemy XIII to Alexandria to explain in person about the current situation in Egypt, Pothinus decided that it befitted the royal dignity for the Pharaoh to arrive at Alexandria accompanied by Achillas and his army. This army numbered some 20,000 men and therefore outnumbered Caesar's men by about five to one even before their 2,000 cavalry were included. The Egyptian force Caesar described as 'not contemptible in their numbers or quality, nor in their experience of warfare'. However, in every other way Caesar certainly felt that his opponents were contemptible, in that even those Romans among them – remnants of the garrison of Gabinius – had been corrupted by their long stay in Alexandria.

> The soldiers of Gabinius had become accustomed to the decadent ways of life in Alexandria, taken wives and fathered numerous offspring, in the process forgetting the discipline and indeed the very name of Romans. As well as these the army had accumulated bandits from Syria and pirates from Cilicia and elsewhere in the region. Runaway slaves from Roman territory were certain of finding sanctuary in Alexandria, on condition that they enrolled in the army. If any owner did attempt to retrieve his property the soldiers banded together to prevent it, reckoning that an attack on one of them was an attack on them all, since almost every one of them was guilty of something.
>
> This was the army that could call for the execution of friends of the royal family, who plundered the property of the rich and laid siege to the royal palace if they wanted a pay rise. As the Alexandrian army had long been accustomed to do, these men were capable of driving one man from the throne and finding another to replace him.
>
> (Caesar, *Civil Wars* 3.110)

Caesar had summoned not only Ptolemy XIII to a personal conference but also his sister Cleopatra. Since the entire Ptolemaic army was now approaching Alexandria, and the city was still under the control of Pothinus and his co-conspirator, Theodotus, it was highly dangerous for young Cleopatra to approach. Yet approach she must, since otherwise only Ptolemy and his advisors would have Caesar's ear. It certainly did not help Cleopatra's cause at the beginning that she had decided that her best course was to side unequivocally with the Romans. She knew from the experience of her father that Roman power was the most certain way of keeping her throne. Therefore, when orders arrived from Caesar to disband her army, she seems promptly to have done so.

This turned out to be an embarrassing mistake, both for Caesar and his loyal subordinate queen. Ptolemy's advisors had no intention of abandoning the military force that was keeping them in power and once Cleopatra's army was quite unnecessarily dissolved there remained no military force in Egypt equal to that of Ptolemy and his advisors. All that Cleopatra had left was her loyalty to Caesar – and she would have to get to him to demonstrate that.

Although only around eighteen years old, Cleopatra had grown up fast – as was highly necessary for any later Ptolemy with ambitions of making it into adulthood. She was ferociously intelligent and extremely ambitious – unsurprisingly so, since as a Ptolemy the only way she could be safe from arbitrary execution at the whim of the ruler was to be that ruler herself. As an expert politician, Cleopatra had also ensured that she was popular with the Egyptian people, and indeed was the first Ptolemy to have learned the native language. Cleopatra's first language was Greek and, like almost all Roman aristocrats of his day, Caesar was fluent in Greek, so he and Cleopatra would have no trouble communicating – if only Cleopatra could get to Caesar in order to communicate with him.

Given the nature of palace politics, it was natural that Cleopatra would have carefully developed contacts within the palace of Alexandria, and she used these to put a dramatic plan into effect. First, she left her army to disband itself and then set out for Alexandria smuggled aboard a small fishing boat. Once ashore in the hostile city she met the agents with whom she had arranged the next step of her plan. Exactly how Cleopatra got into the palace is not fully explained – by the biographer Plutarch's account she was smuggled in along with a sackful of bedlinen. The idea that she was unrolled before Caesar in a presentation carpet is a later fiction.

It is more probable that when she reached Caesar's quarters Cleopatra took the time to arrange herself in a more queenly manner before presenting herself. What Caesar made of his unexpected visitor one can only surmise, for Caesar himself omits any mention of their meeting in his description of events in Alexandria. At the very least he would have found the Egyptian queen intriguing.

> She was an extremely beautiful woman who at that time was in her youthful prime. As well as striking looks she had a charming voice and knew how to make herself an ideal companion. Being beautiful to behold and hear ... she placed all her hopes for the throne in her person and her body, intending to appear before him [Caesar] as both a majestic queen and pitiful supplicant.
> (Cassius Dio, *History* 42.34)

This description somewhat flatters Cleopatra if Plutarch is to be believed. Dio was writing almost two centuries after Cleopatra's death and already her legend was distorted by propaganda and the febrile imaginations of writers who had spent too much time alone with their scrolls. In later eras, and especially by the time Shakespeare had done with her, Cleopatra the *femme fatale* who used her personal magnetism to twist the course of history had largely replaced the competent and unscrupulous ruler that she actually was.

Contemporary coins from Egypt show a different Cleopatra – yet the distinctly plain figure with a large nose and jutting chin who appears on the coinage is also a propaganda figment. Cleopatra needed to present herself to her people as a mature, competent individual personally in charge of Egyptian affairs rather than as a bimbo at the service of Roman leaders, and for that purpose an unattractive portrayal was helpful. The truth may lie somewhere in between:

> We are not told that she possessed beauty beyond compare, or indeed that her looks particularly impressed those who saw her. Yet closer acquaintance revealed an irresistible charm and a fascinating conversationalist. Her voice was like a many-stringed

instrument which she could use in whatever language she pleased, sweet in tone and persuasive in discourse. Her behaviour and character were somehow stimulating.

(Plutarch, *Antony* 27)

It seems reasonably certain that, while the meeting between Caesar and Cleopatra started off with a discussion of politics, things eventually moved to a much more personal level. Certainly, Caesar would have had no inhibitions about the fact that he was married at the time. From the Roman perspective, the purpose of fidelity in marriage was to ensure that the couple produced children of their own bloodline. It was generally clear who was giving birth to a child, so motherhood was pretty well established from the start. Fatherhood was more dubious, and the only way it could be definitely established was if the woman had only one sex partner – her husband. Therefore, Roman wives were expected to be faithful but their husbands were not.

Caesar already had a reputation for sexual promiscuity – his troops referred to him as their 'bald whore-monger' and advised people to lock away their womenfolk while he was in town. His senatorial enemies called him 'every woman's man and every man's woman' – a reference to a supposed affair he had in his youth with King Nicomedes of Bithynia. If this were so, then Caesar eventually had sexual liaisons with two queens and one king (the other being a north African queen in a later campaign) as well as several females of the Roman nobility. One such paramour was Lollia, the wife of that Gabinius whose ex-legionary garrison were now plaguing Egypt. Therefore, it is not far-fetched to believe that for Caesar the meeting with Cleopatra was a case of lust at first sight.

From Cleopatra's point of view Caesar had a lot to offer. While there has been considerable speculation as to how sexually experienced she was at that point, young Cleopatra probably found somewhat flattering the interest of the charming, extremely rich conqueror of most of the known world. Even if that were not the case (Caesar was literally old enough to be Cleopatra's father), there was certainly a lot to be said for closing her eyes and thinking of Egypt. Rome had a recent history of deciding who ruled Egypt, and at the moment Caesar ruled Rome. If sex with Caesar was the price of the Egyptian throne Cleopatra was certainly prepared to pay it. And after all, was an evening of sex not less obscene than sacrificing the lives of her supporters for the same purpose?

When the next morning arrived Ptolemy XIII arrived at the court to present his case to Caesar. He had not expected to discover that his sister was already there and behaving towards Caesar in a manner which left little doubt about their relationship. Under the circumstances, Ptolemy could be excused for believing that he was unlikely to get a fair hearing. Reports claim that the furious young pharaoh threw his diadem to the ground, called his sister a number of names (of which 'traitor' was among the more polite) and stormed out of the meeting.

Caesar does not describe what happened next, but from later events it became clear that Caesar simply refused to take 'no' as an answer. In his will Ptolemy Auletes had appointed his two elder children as joint heirs to Egypt, and joint heirs Ptolemy and Cleopatra would be, even if one were a puppet sat upon his throne by force and the other spent more time sitting in Caesar's lap.

To the public a somewhat different story was presented, and in a hurry. The Alexandrian gossip machine quickly spread the word that their pharaoh was being held captive by Caesar and the city reacted violently to the news. A mob quickly assembled which threatened to storm the palace and overwhelm the tiny force that Caesar had at his command. Caesar did the only thing he could – he stepped out and addressed the outraged population.

He put their fears at rest by assuring them of what was 'really' happening. In Caesar's version of the truth, Ptolemy and Cleopatra had been reconciled by his benevolent arbitration and were now putting their differences aside. Caesar read out the will of Ptolemy

Auletes which had left the kingdom jointly to Cleopatra and Ptolemy and announced that the two would henceforth work harmoniously for the good of their country and its people. A large banquet had been arranged to celebrate this happy outcome.

The mob were appeased by the apparent return to amity between their co-rulers and gradually dispersed. While organizing his banquet to celebrate the return of peace, Caesar also set his legionaries to frantically fortifying the palace district. If it eventually dawned on the Alexandrians that Caesar had pulled the wool over their eyes, the Romans would in future be more prepared to hold off another onslaught.

Among those definitely not fooled by Caesar's honeyed words was Pothinus. He had briefly tried to oil his way into Caesar's circle, but lacked the charm, youth and gender of Cleopatra. Caesar had brushed his overtures aside with the observation that, given the state of the country, he saw no use for Egyptian advisors – a comment which left Pothinus excluded from the position of power which he felt was his due. Like his protégé, young Ptolemy, Pothinus was free to leave the palace any time he chose, so long as he did not actually set foot outside the door. Not unexpectedly, his response was to smile bravely despite his changed fortune, and to secretly urge Achillas to bring his army to the palace and dispose of both the traitorous Cleopatra and her annoying Roman lover with all possible expediency.

However, Caesar was not naïve enough to leave Pothinus unwatched, and his own spy (his personal barber, according to Plutarch), doubtless with the help of Cleopatra's own agents, quickly discovered the plot. Indeed, one might cynically imagine that they would have discovered the plot even if there had not been a plot to find. Pothinus was executed less for conspiracy than because he was dangerous, surplus to requirements and one of the murderers of Pompey. He had to go, and the highly credible accusation that he was conspiring against the new Egyptian order was a good way to dispose of him. (Theodotus, the man who had originally proposed the murder of Pompey had already seen the writing on the wall and expeditiously vanished. He was found years later in Asia Minor where the Roman governor – Cassius, yet again – had him brutally tortured to death.)

Achillas had either never left the camp of the Egyptian army or had escaped back to it. He had few illusions about his fate as an enemy of Cleopatra and the killer of Pompey, and was not inclined to surrender to Caesar the one bargaining chip in his possession – his army. Caesar made the attempt anyway by sending messengers to the camp of Achillas ordering him that, if he was not prepared to stand down to at least keep the fragile peace. It was perhaps a misjudgement of Caesar's to send the messengers not in his own name but in that of the now-captive Ptolemy XIII. Achillas hardly needed a moment to recognize the hand of Caesar operating through the guise of a command from his pharaoh, and responded with a mixture of contempt and indignation.

Achillas called together his troops and denounced the messengers before them, pointing out that Caesar's transparent attempt to keep the peace was in fact proof of the weakness of the Romans and the panic of their commander. Achillas accompanied this speech with a denunciation of Cleopatra so effective that in the end the envoys from Caesar were lynched by the soldiery.

Since Ptolemy XIII had been transferred from being his figurehead to being Caesar's, Achillas sent messengers to the last available Ptolemy, young Arsinoe, and informed her that he was now campaigning in her name to free Egypt from foreign domination. With this noble cause foremost in his propaganda message to the Alexandrians, Achillas began military operations. Thus, sometime in late 48 BC, the Alexandrian War got formally under way.

At this point we should take a moment to admire the enormity of Caesar's blunder. At the time of Caesar's arrival in Egypt, Cleopatra and her brother Ptolemy XIII had been fighting a lively little civil war. Both had armies under their command – Ptolemy the Egyptian army, Cleopatra a force composed largely of mercenaries and soldiers of fortune. Caesar had arrived in Egypt with barely an army of his own, but took it upon himself to decide how the civil war was to be brought to an end, after which he would pronounce upon who would rule Egypt.

Caesar ordered both sides to stand down their armies, even though he had no way of enforcing that order. The result, naturally enough, was that only those prepared to obey Caesar – his potential allies – disbanded the very forces that he was going to desperately need to fight off the soldiers led by those who were not prepared to obey him. Cleopatra had disbanded her army, and therefore had nothing but her loyalty to offer. Yet after he had slept with Cleopatra, Caesar made it plain that his new bedmate would be running things in Egypt thereafter.

If one is going to pick the winner of a civil war, then it is best to begin matters with an idea of which side you are going to pick. Yet, after one night of passion, Caesar chose Cleopatra, who had already obeyed Caesar's order to disband her own army. This left only one substantial army in the country – that of the disappointed Ptolemy XIII, whose supporters were quite willing to use force to express their disagreement with Caesar's choice.

If Caesar had decided to support Cleopatra before he had sex with her, then telling her to disband her troops seems odd to say the least. And yet afterwards openly choosing Cleopatra in defiance of the will of the Alexandrians and the will of the only army in the region shows the same arrogant disregard of the consequences as Caesar had already shown since his arrival in the country. One would imagine a more skilled diplomat would have kept both sides hopeful of winning Roman backing until Caesar was in a position to enforce his will by military force.

As it was Caesar had managed to alienate the leaders of the only remaining substantial military force in the country. At the same time Caesar had also quite unnecessarily alienated Ptolemy XIII by his blatant partisanship, and that alienation meant that Caesar had to take the young pharaoh hostage. By doing this Caesar outraged the Alexandrians in whose city he was a guest – a people who had already been infuriated by Caesar's high-handed attitude since he had arrived.

Chapter 5

Battleground Alexandria

Caesar's war in Egypt is called the Alexandrian War because military operations never extended far beyond the city, and mostly took place within it. The average Egyptian peasant living further upstream of the Nile may have heard vague rumours of (yet another) rumpus in Alexandria, but the vast majority of Egyptians were largely unaffected by the clash of armies in the Nile Delta. In fact, the modern historian is probably better informed of events than were the citizens of Egypt at the time.

This largesse of information is mainly due to two sources, one of whom is Julius Caesar himself. Caesar was hardly an unbiased commentator, and many a modern observer has pointed out that not only was Caesar necessarily prejudiced towards himself but his books are skilfully written examples of ancient political propaganda. Nevertheless, given the rarity and unreliability of most sources from ancient history, having a text written by one of the actual protagonists is a true treasure. The other source for events in Alexandria is the writer who produced the essential text for any historian interested in the conflict, the *De Bello Alexandrino* (*The Alexandrine War*).

Although not written by Caesar, *De Bello Alexandrino* is generally lumped in with the Caesarian corpus of writing. It would be very useful to identify the actual author but as early as the second century there were doubts as to who this was. Caesar's biographer Suetonius remarked of the text, 'Of the Alexandrine War … the identity of the writer is uncertain. Some think it was Oppius.'

Although the text was intended as a continuation of Caesar's own work, the author at no point claims to be Caesar, but then Caesar himself does not claim to be Caesar in those texts which he indubitably did write. This was because Caesar disingenuously claimed that he was not writing an account of his wars but merely providing basic notes for later historians to enlarge upon in a 'proper' history. (The fact that no ancient historians took Caesar up on his generous offer shows that these historians were well aware that Caesar's 'notes' were in fact brilliantly written Latin which would be very hard to match and impossible to improve upon.)

It is precisely because the text of *De Bello Alexandrino* is not written in his usual pellucid style that later critics are sure that this was not the work of Caesar himself. In fact, the style resembles that of the author of the eighth book of Caesar's *De Bello Gallico*, who expressly explains that this part of that famous text was not written by Caesar. 'I here append a supplement to the commentary on the operations in Gaul written by our great Caesar.'

The writer elsewhere goes on to explain that he is continuing Caesar's account 'from operations in Alexandria onwards', because Caesar's own description of affairs in Egypt stops abruptly with the commencement of hostilities in Alexandria. This would imply that the same author of the eighth book of the Gallic Wars went on to write *De Bello Alexandrino* and also the accounts of Caesar's subsequent African and Spanish Wars.

Yet few today believe this to be the case. While the descriptions of two of the wars – the Spanish and African – fall well below the quality of Caesar's own writing, they are each substandard in their own way. Yet much of the writing has a first-hand feel which belies the author's claim that 'Fortune determined that I should take no part in the Alexandrian or African campaigns', but that he did have the benefit of interviewing Caesar extensively on these topics.

So who did actually write the history of the Alexandrian War, when did he write it, and how reliable is the information therein? Suetonius, as we have seen, reckons that the author may have been 'Oppius'. This would be Gaius Oppius, an intimate friend of Caesar who looked after his personal affairs in Rome while Caesar was away on campaign, and who remained close to Caesar until the latter's assassination. Certainly, Oppius was a skilled writer who produced a number of other works, including a biography of Caius Marius and another of Scipio Africanus.

Unfortunately for his credibility as a historian, Oppius was an unashamed partisan of the Caesarian party. The biographer Plutarch drew upon some of Oppius' work for his own biography of Pompey and remarks that one 'must be very careful not to believe all that he says'. After Caesar's death Oppius transferred his allegiance to Caesar's heir Octavian and put considerable energy into a text refuting the fact that Cleopatra had given birth to Caesar's actual and only son, Caesarion.

Therefore, it is probably something of a relief to discover that most historians believe that while Oppius may have written the *Alexandrine War*, it is more probable that the text was written by another close associate of Caesar, Aulus Hirtius.

If this is the case, we can hardly hope for a better source. Hirtius knew Caesar well – indeed it is alleged that the night that Caesar crossed the Rubicon he dined with Hirtius in his tent. Caesar also spent some time with Hirtius immediately after the Alexandrian War when the two met in Antioch, so some of the anecdotes about Caesar in the text may have come directly from the source. A skilled diplomat, gourmet and writer, Hirtius was certainly capable of writing the text of the *Alexandrine War* – indeed, none other than Cicero speaks highly of his abilities.

That the *Alexandrine War* contains none of the solecisms contained within the texts of the Spanish and African wars suggests that Hirtius may have intended the same technique for all three books. That is, he commissioned the texts from soldiers who had taken part in each campaign and then planned to re-write each to a higher standard. This he accomplished with *De Bello Alexandrino* but he had only got around to lightly editing the other texts due to his own untimely death (in battle against Mark Antony at Mutina in 43 BC).

Therefore in the text of the *Alexandrine War* we have a history of events in Alexandria between 48 and 47 BC. This history was drafted by someone who was probably there at the time and re-written by an author who was thoroughly familiar with the details and who had personally interviewed at least one of the leading characters. As texts from ancient history go, we can seldom do much better that that.

One reassuring detail of the text is that it is accurate in one of the aspects that can still be checked today – the author knew his contemporary Alexandria. Alexandria is one of the best-documented cities of the ancient world after Athens and Rome and modern historians are able to track many of the events in the text to particular streets and districts. These places are where they should have been for internal consistency. Again this suggests that even if Oppius/Hirtius was not present at the time, this text draws very strongly upon the recollections of someone who actually witnessed events at first hand.

In a very real sense the city of Alexandria can be considered as being one of the main protagonists in this history. Just as it has been necessary to untangle the convoluted sequence of events which brought Caesar, Cleopatra and Ptolemy XIII together in Alexandria, before we can fully understand what happened in this brief-but-nasty little war, it is also necessary to understand how Alexandria itself got to be where and what it was.

Perhaps the most important point is that despite its location, Cleopatra's Alexandria was not an Egyptian city. Nor despite the efforts of generations of Ptolemies to make it so, was it entirely a Greek city, though it was probably more Greek than anything else. This identity crisis was not unique to Alexandria, but shared with a number of Greek cities that were scattered around the Mediterranean and well beyond. (Few today for example know that the city of Kandahar in Afghanistan was also once an 'Alexandria', taking its name from the local form of Alexander, which was 'Iskandar'.) Like all cities outside the Greek mainland, while Alexandria strove hard to remain Hellenistic, indigenous culture generally found some way of permeating the urban society. As a trading port and Egyptian capital, Alexandria rapidly became more cosmopolitan than the average Greek 'colony'.

Alexandria was not the only city which Greek colonists had founded in Egypt after the Macedonian conquest, but it was by far the greatest. It owed its greatness both directly and indirectly to Alexander the Great, who personally founded the place in 331 or 332 BC. (The exact date is uncertain.)

Like many of Alexander's foundations, Alexandria was not a completely new settlement, as so ideal a site on the Nile delta could not reasonably have been expected to have been unoccupied. There was apparently an Egyptian town called Rhakotis already established, though most of this settlement did not survive the attentions of Alexander's city planners. While a number of fanciful tales have survived of Alexander's role in the foundation, it is probable that the busy Alexander did little more than approve the site and settle other matters outstanding in Egypt before rushing off to conquer the rest of the civilized world. (Rome to the west was not yet considered to have earned the apellation of 'civilized'.)

Nevertheless, the remit given to those awarded the task of actually taking Alexandria from an idea to a functioning city certainly allowed them to think big. Alexandria was not to be yet another of the many Alexandriae which were scattered like confetti through the lands conquered by Macedon – *this* Alexandria was meant to be Alexander's greatest memorial. As such it was imagined on a grand scale and from the beginning constructed accordingly.

For a start Alexandria was a symbol of the new Egypt. This was to be an outward-looking nation connected to the rest of the Mediterranean world, rather than the self-contained Egypt of yore which had its capital at Memphis, hundreds of kilometres up the Nile. The new capital was to be Greek, a mercantile as well as an administrative centre, and not merely another Greek colony but the greatest beacon of Hellenistic culture anywhere, including in mainland Greece itself.

Alexander never saw the realization of his grand dream, for he never returned to the city before his death in Babylon almost a decade later. However, even before he founded the city he had given it a great start in life by his destruction of the Phoenician city of Tyre. Tyre, in the years before Alexander comprehensively flattened it, had been one of the major western termini of that trade route that later came to be known as the Silk Road. Alexandria was intended not only to replace Tyre in this role, but to far surpass it.

The city was well-located for this purpose. It was situated on the Nile Delta close enough to the sea for it to be a Mediterranean port. However, it was not so far from the Red Sea that goods from the east could not be transported overland with relative ease – especially as the first Ptolemies imported from Alexander's eastern conquests an animal ideally suited for packing goods across desert terrain. This animal was the camel, which had been unknown in Egypt until then.

Greek emissaries had long been in contact with their counterparts in India, and soon enterprising merchants had worked out how to create a southern leg of the Silk Road that took goods from the Orient across India to be shipped to the Mediterranean.

Not long after the foundation of Alexandria, daring navigators discovered a trick that greatly speeded up the shipment of goods. Rather than hug the shores of the Red Sea and Persian Gulf, a ship bound for India could sail boldly right out into the Arabian sea. If they did this in the early spring, they would be caught by the prevailing northeasterly monsoon winds and carried to India in a matter of weeks instead of months as previously.

Then, in October, the system reverses itself and cool dry air blows from the Himalayas across the ocean towards Africa. This system meant that a merchant could carry goods to India, spend a few months haggling in the bazaars and then catch a ride back to Alexandria all in the same year, crossing the ocean in less time than it took to traverse the Mediterranean, although the trip was twice the distance. As a result, visitors to a market in Alexandria could find Ethiopians trading gold and ivory products, Yemenis offering frankincense and myrrh, and Indians with stocks of Malaysian pepper and nutmeg.

Unlike their debauched and degenerate descendants, the early Ptolemies realized the opportunity for the aggrandizement of their city and seized it with both hands. The money from trade combined with the inherent wealth of Egypt to allow for grand projects, the first of which was the construction of Alexandria itself. While named for Alexander, the city was in fact the creation of one Dinocrates, the leading professional city-planner of the Hellenistic era.

Alexandria was founded on a long narrow limestone ridge edged on the north by the sea with a large lake called Mareotis to the south. Therefore the main roads of the city ran in a straight line from east to west, intersected at right angles by roads running north to south. This grid plan was tilted slightly off true north both because of the angle of the limestone ridge and because Dinocrates wanted the prevailing winds to blow right across the city down the wide streets which ran directly from one city gate to the other.

Another advantage of building a city from scratch is that as well as roads, one can get other aspects of the infrastructure just right. One of these aspects was what would have been another of the wonders of the ancient world, if more people had got to see it. This was a system of cisterns put into place before the first buildings were erected above them. 'Cisterns' is perhaps an inadequate word for these reservoirs, which even two thousand years later were so magnificent that an awed Victorian travel writer referred to them as 'underground cathedrals'. This guaranteed the citizens a constant supply of fresh water – though as Caesar was to discover, they did not guarantee a supply of water during a siege.

The water for the reservoirs came from a canal which ran between Lake Mareotis and the city. At one point this canal spilled over into a marsh which extended northwards roughly dividing the city in two, with a mainly Jewish sector to the east and the Greeks and native Egyptians in a larger section to the west.

As Greek rulers in a foreign land it had occurred to the first Ptolemies that they might not always be popular with their subjects – or with each other. Therefore, the Royal Palace was actually a complex consisting of three discrete buildings built on the Lachias Promontory, a narrow finger of land which reached northward to make up the eastern horn of the Great Harbour of Alexandria. This site was easily separated from the rest of the city, especially as the marsh which almost divided the city stretched northwards to within half a mile of the base of the Lachias Promontory. In short the palace complex was highly defensible – a precaution that Caesar was greatly to appreciate.

Looking west across the Great Harbour Caesar could have seen the Heptastadion, a gigantic causeway (seven times longer than a stadium, hence the name) linking the city to the island of Pharos. So much maritime traffic did Alexandria handle that there was another port on the other side of the causeway called the 'Old Port' (Eunostos).

Pharos was the location of Alexandria's iconic lighthouse, one of the Wonders of the ancient world, and the reason why 'faro' is the word for lighthouse in several modern languages (including Italian). The lighthouse is almost certainly the first thing Caesar saw of Alexandria, as it was visible for miles out to sea, all the more so because it is believed a mirror was mounted at the top to serve the same purpose as a light at night. However, there was probably also a fire lit in the day, because while a light serves as a beacon at night, a column of smoke could double the height of the 350 ft (105m) tower. Apart from another of the Wonders, (the Great Pyramid at Giza) the lighthouse was the tallest structure of its day and was to remain so for centuries to come.

As with all the great accomplishments of Ptolemaic Egypt, the lighthouse had been built in the early days of the dynasty, and when Caesar saw it the structure was already well over two hundred years old. So well was it constructed that the lighthouse would stand for another millennium before being felled by an earthquake in AD 1303.

Another of the great treasures of Alexandria was the famous Library. 'Library' is something of an understatement for this building complex which was the major centre of scholarship in the ancient world. It was situated in the Rhakotis district not far from the warehouses and docks on the mainland side of the Heptastadion causeway. The early Ptolemies had aggressively built up the library by collecting texts from everywhere in the ancient world. Famously, scrolls were confiscated from ships docking at the harbour and taken to the Library for copying. If the text was considered significant, the library kept the original and returned the copy.

Under the tutelage of the later Ptolemies, the Library had gone into something of a decline. Its reputation as the leading centre of scholarship in the Mediterranean world never recovered from Ptolemy VIII. He, in 145 BC, decided that the intellectuals at the Library were opposed to his rule and conducted a savage purge that probably cost the life of the head librarian (among others) while most of the remaining scholars were driven into exile. The Library continued to operate, and with the help of its unparalleled resources Alexandria was to remain a scientific centre. Caesar, who was something of an intellectual, may have visited the Library in the days while he was waiting for Egypt's warring pharaohs, Cleopatra and Ptolemy XIII, to show up.

Another sight which Caesar would have been keen to see was the corpse of Alexandria's founder, great Alexander himself. Alexander had left the city as a set of plans awaiting realization and never saw it again in his life. Nevertheless, Alexandria had plenty of opportunities to see Alexander after his death, because the first Ptolemy hijacked the body as it was being taken from Babylon to Macedon for burial. Possession of Alexander's corpse was one of the ways that Ptolemy had signalled that he intended Egypt to be dominant in the Hellenistic world. Now, apart from Egypt, the Hellenistic world no longer existed, having either fallen apart after dynastic struggles or been subsumed by the growing power of Rome.

In the eyes of Ptolemy's supporters Egypt itself was now also under threat. Egypt's queen was – probably literally – under Caesar. The other pharaoh was a prisoner and the country's fate was in the hands of a Roman warlord. There remained one chance for sovereignty, and that lay in the fact that Caesar had, with typical rashness, arrived in Alexandria with a puny force.

Were the Egyptians to destroy both Caesar and Cleopatra before Caesar could bring in reinforcements from abroad, then it was very possible that Caesar's enemies might win the civil war after all. Without Caesar as the driving force his rebellion would splutter out, and the Roman Republic might be restored. In such circumstances the Roman Senate might be prepared to overlook the murder of Pompey (with whom the aristocracy had only allied out of necessity) and restore to Egypt its autonomy.

This noble ideal elevated what had been a squalid power struggle between rival siblings into a nationalist cause. Certainly, when the matter was put to them like that the people of Alexandria immediately sided with Ptolemy. Or more accurately they sided with Arsinoe, because Ptolemy was in the palace complex as a captive of Caesar. (In fact Caesar had young Ptolemy stand on the walls outside the palace and deliver a pro-Caesar speech, which the Alexandrians totally disregarded, divining correctly that Ptolemy had been coerced into giving it.) In any case, for the Alexandrians the crucial issue was not whose side they were on, that of Ptolemy or Arsinoe, but who they were against. And they were against Caesar. Hostilities began almost immediately.

> With abundant supplies and high productivity the city was a ready source of [war] materiel. The people themselves were quick and cunning. As soon as they saw what we were doing they reproduced it so skilfully that the version produced by our

troops seemed to be the imitation – and they came up with other devices of their own as well. ... In meeting after meeting their leaders repeatedly stressed why they were doing this.

'The Romans have been annexing our kingdom bit by bit over the years. Gabinius came here with his army. Then Pompey came here as a fugitive, and now Caesar has followed with his men. Even with Pompey gone, Caesar has remained and shows no inclination to leave. If he is not driven out Egypt is doomed to become a Roman province. And the time to defeat him is now, while the seasonal storms have closed the sea to reinforcements from abroad.'

(Alexandrine War 3)

Chapter 6

The Opening Rounds

The outbreak of hostilities came as no surprise to Caesar who was well aware that his vulnerability made him a tempting target for aggression. He had at most 4,000 men with him, while the Egyptian army was at least five times larger – even before the bellicose population of Alexandria was included among his enemies. From the moment he landed in Alexandria, Caesar would have been aware of his peril.

Pompey had been a defeated general, but he had been still the leader of the Republican side in a civil war that was far from over. Yet, despite the threat of retaliation if the Republican side did eventually prevail, the Egyptians had killed him anyway. And while Caesar was now in the ascendant, he was still considered by many as a rebel general in arms against the legal government of Rome. If Caesar were also to be killed in Egypt there was no immediate successor to pick up the torch, and indeed no cause for Caesar's men to die for – Caesar himself was the reason for the civil war, and with his death his armies would have nothing to fight for. In other words, if the Egyptians did kill Caesar they would probably go unpunished.

In short, the Egyptians had as good a reason to kill Caesar as they had previously for killing Pompey and grounds at least as solid for believing that they could get away with it. These were the grim facts that would have been grasped by Caesar the moment he saw the severed head of Pompey. It is an interesting question whether Caesar would have chosen this moment to make an expeditious retreat from Egypt had he been able so to do. On the one hand, the winds from the north were already making problematic the departure of his little fleet, but on the other hand the Egyptians were so keen to see him go that they would have probably towed his ships offshore themselves had he but asked.

Instead, Caesar had acted with typical boldness. Rather than show any signs of fear he had acted imperiously almost from the start, as the head of the mighty Roman state come to impose his will upon an obedient client kingdom. For this reason he had ordered his lictors to carry through Alexandria the fasces that symbolized his status as dictator of Rome. This act was deliberately provocative and provided a test for Caesar as to what extent the Alexandrians were prepared to accept his authority.

The subsequent civil unrest resulted in the death of several of Caesar's men. This would have clearly demonstrated to Caesar his low standing with the average Alexandrian citizen, but nevertheless he pressed on. He announced that while he was in Egypt he intended to collect outstanding monies owed by the Egyptians to Rome, to the tune of some 10,000,000 denarii. Then, reading publicly to the Alexandrians the will of Ptolemy Auletes, Caesar had announced that he would be the final arbiter of who ruled the country.

In short then, Caesar had gambled. He had hoped that in acting as though his authority was unchallengeable, it would not be challenged – and he almost got away with it. However, Caesar was a poor politician. It is necessary to state this explicitly as many in later generations have assumed rather the opposite, basing their opinion on the fact that Caesar did in fact successfully take over the Roman Republic. However, this assumes that Caesar's ambition all along was to achieve supreme power and overthrow the Republic, whereas, apart from the propaganda claims of his enemies, there is little evidence for this intention.

Given his many advantages – birth into an up-and-coming family, natural charisma and high intelligence – Caesar should have anyway risen naturally to the top of Rome's political elite. Instead, from his late teens he seemed to go out of the way to make enemies and alienate people – to the extent that, once he had politically painted himself in to a corner with the expiration of his command in Gaul, the enemies he had made in the Senate hated him so much that they were prepared to abandon constitutional procedure in order to bring him down.

It should go without saying that good politicians do not have to take power by leading an armed insurrection against their own government, especially when – as we have seen – that insurrection was a gamble which came very close to coming unstuck in Greece. Furthermore, as Augustus later demonstrated, a skilled politician could seize power in a military coup and still die in bed rather than finish his career perforated by the daggers of his fellow senators in the ultimate no-confidence vote.

Therefore, it should come as no surprise that, in executing Pothinus, imprisoning Ptolemy XIII and openly siding with Cleopatra, Caesar had toppled off the political tightrope he had been hoping to tread. He was now instead compelled to do what he did best, which was resolve matters by military force.

Had Caesar always intended to resolve matters by force, he would have brought that force with him and he would not have been so quick to order Cleopatra to his presence when she could have been much more usefully employed as an ally leading her army against Achillas. As it was, Caesar had now to send urgently for reinforcements while preparing the men he had on hand to withstand a brutal siege until those reinforcements arrived. Given his shortage of manpower and the open hostility of the Alexandrian population, there was no question of Caesar holding the city as a whole against the advancing Egyptian army.

Fortunately he did not have to. While the later Ptolemies were mostly child-kings or debauched nonentities wholly occupied with lethal palace politics, the first Ptolemy and his immediate successors had been excellent rulers. Like any cautious politicians, the early Ptolemies had not taken for granted the goodwill of the people they ruled. Consequently, the palace section of Alexandria was sited with defence in mind. It also had its own private harbour to allow for the safe arrival of reinforcements or to allow a convenient escape by water if things got really desperate. (Few in today's democratic Britain realize that their Houses of Parliament are built right on the banks of the River Thames for that same reason.)

Caesar claims that on his arrival in Alexandria he had been allocated a house to serve as his residence while he was in the capital. If this was the case then the Egyptian authorities had been somewhat remiss in providing Caesar with accommodation that he says was easily converted into a fortress. The surrounding streets were easily secured and once this had been done Caesar had free access to the various docks and mini-harbours of the peninsula. There is also the possibility that the Alexandrians had not been this generous. Instead, it may be that Caesar, who had been well aware of the potential for trouble the moment he had landed at Alexandria, had simply located the house best suited for his needs on the peninsula and illegally and arbitrarily requisitioned it from the occupants – a fact that he might have been reluctant to share with readers of his often-disingenuous account of the civil wars.

Not only was the area of the palace complex surrounded by sea on three sides, but the entire land area – called the Lachias Promontory – was a long, narrow spit easily defended by a relatively small number of men. Nor was this the only advantage. If the worse came to the worst and Caesar and his men were defeated even here, they could retreat by sea to a small island nearby in the harbour called the Antirhodos. There were a number of royal buildings on this island, which was only a few hundred hectares in area (about a thousand acres) and therefore eminently defensible.

Accordingly, Caesar sent to Greece for his troops and sent messengers to client kings of nearby places such as Pergamon and Nabatea demanding immediate assistance. He set about procuring the services of the mercenary archers for which the island of Crete was famous. With the Egyptian side not prepared even to open negotiations, Caesar realized that he had done all he could for now; at present the initiative rested with the enemy.

Achillas firmly seized that initiative. Given that some of his veteran troops were ex-Roman legionaries, he felt confident that these men would give a good account of themselves in the bitter street fighting that lay ahead. Therefore, on arrival at Alexandria he plunged straight into the city and attempted to master the entire place by storm. Caesar had expected no less and taken the appropriate precautions, including, as we have seen, concentrating his soldiers at the base of the promontory containing the palace complex. Caesar's troops were not just veterans but also battle-hardened from the recent campaign in Greece. The Gabinian legionaries of Achillas were held in check; in fact there is reason to suspect that to some extent the street battle was a diversion intended to tie up Caesar's troops while the real aim of Achillas' attack was to gain control of the harbour.

The prize in the harbour was the fleet which Caesar had been painfully accumulating. This consisted of the ships he had brought with him and other ships which he had seized on their way to support the recently deceased Pompey. There were twenty-two ships of the Alexandrian fleet which Caesar had commandeered early in the proceedings and, as an extra bonus, fifty Egyptian ships which had gone to support the Republican army in the Pharsalus campaign. After Caesar's victory in Thessaly these ships had returned home and fallen straight into Caesar's welcoming arms.

There were triremes, quadremes and quinqueremes, reports Caesar mournfully, all beautifully kitted out and ready to put to sea at a moment's notice. No wonder that Achillas lusted after these ships and attacked the harbour in overwhelming force. If he could gain control of the fleet he would be master of the Levantine seaboard and control all access to the Nile Delta. Not only would Caesar have no means of retreat, but even if he continued to hold out on the Lachias promontory Achillas would have a noose around his neck.

For a start, while Caesar's men were holding back the Egyptian army at the base of the promontory, they did not have a lot of manpower to spare. With his superior numbers and control of the ships from the fleet, Achillas could pin Caesar's legionaries with an attack on the landward side and simultaneously open up another front or two by landing troops elsewhere on the promontory.

Even if that proved ineffective (given the changes in the shoreline there is now no way of knowing how easy it was to land troops on the Lachias peninsula in Caesar's day) Achillas could still win the long game. With the Egyptians already in control of the land, gaining control of access to the harbour meant that there was no way for supplies to reach Caesar's besieged forces. Furthermore, all those reinforcements which Caesar had requested from across the eastern Mediterranean must either fight their way in from Gaza or simply stay at home once Achillas had a fleet with which to keep them from reaching Caesar.

If Achillas secured the ships the war would be over almost as soon as it started – a fact that was manifestly clear to the soldiers on both sides. This led to very intense fighting, because the army of Achillas wanted nothing more than to get the siege over with as soon as possible, while Caesar's men were well aware that if they lost the ships they also lost their only hope of survival. The outcome of the fight quickly became clear – Caesar's men were far from outmatched, but they were heavily outnumbered. There was no way of stopping the Egyptians from getting to the ships, but Caesar could still deny them their prize. Accordingly, and doubtless with bitter reluctance, he ordered that the ships should be burned. Nor could it have done much for the morale of Caesar's legionaries to set about destroying the ships which, but for a contrary wind, could have carried them to safety over a fortnight ago.

Caesar does not mention that this action at the docks not only set the fleet ablaze, but also several nearby buildings. These included the grain warehouses that he relied upon for rations for his legions, and which Achillas might have deliberately destroyed. Of little strategic value but to the great annoyance of future historians, the famed library of Alexandria was part of the collateral damage. It is unknown how much of the library was destroyed, and the institution was certainly fully functional for centuries afterwards, but the fact that every contemporary historian (except Caesar) mentions this fire suggests that the damage was significant.

In setting his fleet ablaze Caesar had literally burned his boats. Not all of his fleet had gone up in smoke, but he had certainly lost enough to make it impossible to transport large numbers of men. He still had the option of leaving Alexandria once the wind changed but at the cost of leaving his men behind.

A later inventory (given in *Alexandrine War* 13) gives the details of the ships still remaining under Caesar's control. The main strike force was nine Rhodian warships remaining of those which had come with him to Alexandria (others had been lost at sea or on the coast), eight Pontic ships, twelve from Pergamon in Asia Minor and five from Lycia (also in Asia Minor, and crewed by people with a strong nautical tradition). Of these only about a dozen ships had covered decks – ie they were triremes or quinqueremes, the main combat ships of the time.

For the present, all Caesar could do with the tactical flotilla he still had at his disposal was evacuate his men from the harbour area and await reinforcements. In a typically deft move, Caesar combined these two objectives by loading his men into his unburned ships and evacuating them across the harbour to the island of Pharos. He captured one part of the island, where, according to one source, his men killed the inhabitants (whom Caesar says were a bunch of pirates in any case). This was probably the part containing the Lighthouse, which was of great tactical and strategic value.

The Great Lighthouse stood at the end of a causeway that linked it to the mainland. As Caesar explains, the island dominated approaches to the harbour so that whoever was in possession of Pharos could control maritime traffic to Alexandria. Doubtless Caesar's strategic priority was to keep that access open for ships carrying in supplies and his desperately-needed reinforcements. Nevertheless, it would also do no harm to strangle trade and the arrival of goods to the main port as a way of reminding the Alexandrians that their hostility had consequences.

As his attack on the fleet had demonstrated, Achillas was also keenly aware of the role sea power would play in the war. That he had been unable to secure Caesar's fleet was a definite setback, even if he had forced his opponent to destroy the greater part of it. For the moment he had somewhat fewer ships than Caesar, but this was a situation he was evidently determined to rectify at speed. Almost from that moment onward the Egyptian commanders set about commandeering anything that floated, ordering other ships to report in from outlying harbours up and down the delta, and starting an emergency shipbuilding programme with the enthusiastic help of the Alexandrians.

According to the author of the *Alexandrine War*, the citizens of that city were indeed energetically collaborating with the efforts of Achillas in other ways also. The wealthiest citizens had personally raised and sponsored militias, and the city's reserve of veteran fighting men were prepared as a trained fighting force that could be rushed to wherever the fighting was fiercest. Meanwhile the streets and alleys on the landward side of the royal complex were walled off with full-scale blocks of dressed stone, and towers up to ten storeys tall were situated at strategic locations. In case any of these strategic locations had been overlooked, other towers were constructed on wheels so that they, like the reserve veteran squads, could be brought to bear where needed.

At the same time, the Alexandrians made use of their local knowledge to make life uncomfortable for Caesar. It has been previously mentioned that there was a veritable underground river network beneath Alexandria by which the water of the Nile was diverted into huge cisterns, which yielded a supply of fresh water to every part of the city. Since the water came from a canal on the Lake Mareotis side of Alexandria, the water supply necessarily had to pass through the rest of the city to reach the palace complex. This was immediately identified as a point of vulnerability which the locals wasted no time in pointing out to the Egyptian commander.

Following an abrupt change of management, that commander was no longer Achillas. He had fallen victim to the unfortunate fact that he and his fellow Egyptians were too addicted to palace intrigue to forswear their deadly games even when facing as serious an enemy as Caesar. In order to rally nationalist sentiment behind him, Achillas had presented himself as a supporter of the only Ptolemy not currently in Caesar's power, namely Cleopatra's younger sister, Arsinoe. Given that he had taken that position, Achillas could hardly object when Arsinoe herself joined his army.

Achillas required of Arsinoe only that she be a figurehead whose mere presence would help to rally the Egyptians behind his cause. Arsinoe promptly made it clear that she possessed the same hands-on attitude to ruling a country as had her sister Cleopatra. Rather than sitting back and submissively allowing Achillas to conduct operations, she at once started telling him what to do. When Achillas objected to being thrust into a subordinate role, Arsinoe promptly replaced him with her own general – a eunuch called Ganymedes who had formerly been Arsinoe's personal tutor.

Naturally, Arsinoe was aware that Achillas might feel somewhat bitter about being turfed from his command by the very person he had pledged his army to support. Therefore, she took what any of the later Ptolemies would consider the very reasonable precaution of executing her benefactor. Then she made sure that the army would enthusiastically support the new leadership by raising pay and improving conditions.

As a tutor who suddenly had an army to command, Ganymedes proved unexpectedly competent in his new role. Once the Alexandrians had pointed out the issue to him, he immediately set about cutting off the water supply to Caesar's army. This proved unexpectedly difficult as the underground channels were annoyingly numerous and too poorly documented to be simply destroyed. However, these channels all had a common source and this source Ganymedes set about polluting. First, he blocked off those conduits he could and then, using a massive system of hastily built waterwheels, he pumped a huge quantity of seawater into Caesar's supply.

It did not take long before Caesar's soldiers noted that their water was more brackish than previously, and that this undrinkable water was slowly infiltrating the palace supply as it spread underground from building to building. Not unexpectedly this caused considerable consternation, not just among Caesar's men but also among those Alexandrians walled in along with the Romans. Some of these were citizens who genuinely supported Caesar's cause, either out of disaffection for their fellow citizens or because they were gambling that a Roman victory would put them on the winning aside. Others were simply trapped behind the Roman walls by a quirk of city geography, and since only circumstances had forced them on to the Roman side (literally) these citizens were considered far from trustworthy,

Thus, with drinking water running short and the almost certain presence of a fifth column already behind their lines, Caesar's legionaries promptly decided that the time was ripe – indeed overdue – for a speedy evacuation to the island of Antirhodos.

Caesar was less inclined to move. The Antirhodos island was a bolt hole of last resort and Caesar was not prepared to concede that things had yet become that desperate. He therefore called a meeting of the troops and firmly described to his men the risks involved in getting to the island. For a start this obviously required a water crossing, and at this time the Alexandrians controlled the rest of the harbour.

If they saw the Romans taking to the boats they would certainly board anything that floated and attack the Romans en masse with that impromptu fleet. Even if many of the legionaries did reach the island some of their transports would be sunk or captured. (It went without saying that if the legionaries attempted the crossing while wearing armour they would drown if their boat was sunk, and if they did not wear armour they would be all the more vulnerable.) Also, while the Alexandrians had not attempted to seize the island themselves, they would certainly do so if they saw Caesar's men attempting to cross there. Caesar concluded his harangue by stating that his men should put the island out of their minds – in the end they must win or die right where they were.

One reason that Caesar was more sanguine than his panicked men may have been that he was by now a very experienced general. And one of the first things any general did when choosing a fortified position was to check the water supply. While hardly an experienced geologist, Caesar – or some of his staff – would have known that the limestone ridges upon which Alexandria was built were highly permeable. With the lake on one side of the city and the sea on the other there had almost certainly been a natural underground network of fissures and aquifers even before the Alexandrians had constructed a more formal network.

And so it proved. After he had addressed the men, Caesar set his men to digging a number of test wells that very afternoon and they – with understandable enthusiasm – continued digging even after nightfall. With several thousand men actively investigating every promising site with shovels it was almost inevitable that eventually a spring would be located. In fact, the diggers struck a veritable gusher of sweet water, and as the author of the *Alexandrine War* rather smugly remarked, 'And so the painstakingly constructed mechanisms and huge effort of the Alexandrians were made as nothing by a few hours work.'

Chapter 7

The War takes to the Water

So far things had not been going Caesar's way. His trip to Alexandria had been marked by friction with the locals that had flared into open warfare, and an attempt to re-organize the Ptolemaic monarchy that had ended with the two rival rulers as powerless prisoners in their own palace while a third Ptolemy attacked Caesar's outnumbered men with a veteran army.

Once again, Caesar's knack for turning strangers into rabid foes had left him stuck in a pickle largely of his own making. A few weeks previously the Egyptians would have liked nothing more than to see Caesar sail away into the sunset. Now they sought to destroy him and were delighted that he had been forced to burn the very ships that could have gotten him out of Alexandria once the winds changed. Things had definitely been going downhill, and Caesar might justifiably have felt that he was due some good news for a change.

This news duly arrived in a fast boat. (This confirmed Caesar's shrewdness in seizing part of Pharos Island, since otherwise the boat could not have reached him at all.) Aboard were messengers from legionaries sent by one Domitius Calvinus. This Domitius was in some ways Caesar's polar opposite. Where Caesar was a superb general, Domitius was a terrible one. Where Caesar's political decisions tended to land him in hot water (and would ultimately get him killed), Domitius had a talent for ending up on the winning side, and picking that side early.

The messengers brought bad news – namely that while Caesar was trapped in Egypt matters had been getting out of hand elsewhere. For example, Caesar would have been informed that the sons of Pompey had arrived in Spain. Their father had once campaigned successfully in that province and had left behind a considerable reservoir of goodwill for his sons to draw upon. This they had done so effectively that Spain was again in Republican hands. Cato meanwhile had rallied the survivors of Pharsalus and taken them to the province of Africa where he was in the process of forging a formidable army.

Caesar's enemies had also gone east. In Asia Minor they had contacted a disaffected client king called Pharnaces II of Pontus whose father, Mithridates the Great, had once conquered the whole of Anatolia. Pharnaces was now inspired to emulate his father's deeds and promptly went to war with Rome, ostensibly to support the republican cause. War in Asia Minor involved taking on the Roman aristocrat who had early joined the Caesarian side and had been rewarded with command in Asia Minor – Domitius Calvinus. That was the bad news.

The good news was that reinforcements were in the offing. True, the soldiers in the ships now off the coast near Alexandria were not elite legionaries. They were probably elements of Caesar's Legio XXVII and definitely remnants of a legion raised by Pompey for the confrontation at Pharsalus. The latter consisted of troops with sub-optimal training and morale and the men had been sent to serve as garrison troops holding down Asia Minor while the civil war was being wrapped up elsewhere.

Just as important as the transports carrying the troops to Caesar were other ships which Calvinus had packed with corn, artillery and weaponry – also it seems that Calvinus had arranged for water ships to bring in fresh water for the extra men. However, perhaps through haste in dispatching the reinforcements, he had neglected to attach any of these water ships to the present convoy – a failure which was to have significant consequences.

It is not certain whether Calvinus, despite being under pressure from the army of Pharnaces, decided that Caesar's need for soldiers was greater than his own, or whether he had already despatched men and materiel to Egypt before his own domestic emergency developed. Either way, the arrival of these sorely needed reinforcements was a potential game changer if they could only be brought to the Lachias Peninsula in Alexandria where Caesar was holding out.

The problem, yet again, was the winds. These had been for days blowing from the wrong direction and had prevented the ships from reaching the harbour in Alexandria. The fleet had currently found a good anchorage just down the coast and the sailors were now waiting for either a change in the direction of the wind or for fresh orders from Caesar – hence the despatch of the fast boat with the messengers. In response, Caesar decided to examine the situation for himself and set out with his flotilla of surviving warships to personally inspect Calvinus' reinforcements. Caesar took no soldiers with him. Firstly, because there was not enough room on the ships for them all and, secondly, taking his army would mean abandoning Alexandria altogether, and this he was loath to do now that the reinforcements sent by Calvinus gave him a better chance of ultimately prevailing.

The messengers had also wanted to inform Caesar of another problem – the fleet had found a secure anchorage, but there was no water at that site and the lack of water ships meant that supplies were getting dangerously low. Therefore, while on his way to meet his reinforcements Caesar sent foraging parties ashore so that he could meet the fleet with the water they somewhat desperately required. While this was necessary, Caesar's foragers showed a regrettable lack of discipline. They did not stop only to secure a good source of water and load this onto the flotilla, but some adventurous souls ventured further inland looking to pick up plunder from what they supposed to be unguarded enemy territory.

They were proven wrong by an Egyptian cavalry patrol which was deeply interested in what enemy troops were doing so far outside Alexandria. It did not take long for the Egyptians to wring out of the captured foragers the information that Caesar had now left Alexandria and was currently aboard a small fleet without an accompanying army.

This news was promptly relayed back to the Egyptian commanders who acted upon the information as expeditiously as possible.

In the ancient world information and orders travelled as fast as the fastest horse, so the Egyptians knew that they would not be able to reach Caesar before he made contact with his reinforcements. The site where Caesar stopped to take on water has been identified as a promontory some 13km from Alexandria. Once the foragers there had been captured and interrogated and a messenger had informed Ganymedes and Arsinoe that their enemy was outside Alexandria, the pair still had to mobilize whatever ships they had now built or mustered, load these with men and set off in pursuit. All this took time.

It would appear that the wind had abated, for when the impromptu Egyptian fleet did meet up with Caesar he was in the process of bringing his reinforcements back to Alexandria. Nevertheless, even though Caesar's fleet had now joined up with Calvinus' men, the Egyptians were keen on joining battle. The reasoning was probably that it was better to deal with Caesar now, at sea, while his veteran troops were still isolated on the Lachias Peninsula away from the fight. While the Egyptians were ready, willing and able, Caesar was less keen. Firstly, he had fewer troops than the enemy and these men were of untried quality. Secondly, it was already getting near dusk and both sides would be fighting blind.

Not only would Caesar not be able to see how his men were doing, but his men would not be able to see him, and Caesar knew how greatly his presence affected morale. Also, the Egyptians would be less handicapped by the dark because they were fighting on home ground and knew where everything – such as the most dangerous shoals – were in any case. Accordingly, Caesar looked for a defensible point on the coastline where he could beach his ships overnight with a view to reassessing the situation in the morning. Unfortunately, this plan came unstuck almost at the outset.

The problem came from one of the Rhodian ships which had been with Caesar from the beginning of his Alexandrian adventure.

This is somewhat surprising because of all the ships under Caesar's command the Rhodians were the most competent. For centuries ships of the island nation of Rhodes had been a major force in the waters of the eastern Mediterranean. A nation of merchants, the Rhodians had a keen interest in encouraging trade and in keeping down the pirates who fattened upon it. As a result, the Rhodians were probably the best sailors in the Mediterranean and the most expert in naval combat. Roman jealousy of Rhodian naval power had constrained the size of the fleet in recent decades, but what ships the Rhodians still had were of excellent quality, with sailors to match.

Therefore, Caesar found it all the more annoying that it was a Rhodian vessel that had managed to get itself isolated far out on the right-hand side of his flotilla. Nor had only Caesar noted the problem – the Egyptians had done so too and their ships were converging on the Rhodian warship like vultures upon a wounded deer. Four 'decked ships' (i.e. triremes or larger) headed for the vulnerable target, accompanied by a number of smaller craft.

> Caesar was obliged to come to the rescue of the Rhodians – if only to avoid the disgrace of his sailors getting beaten by the enemy in full sight of the rest of his fleet. This, although he reckoned that whatever misfortune should befall the crew, they fully deserved it. (*Alexandrine War* 1.11)

Naval warfare in the Mediterranean had changed somewhat since the days of the Peloponnesian War, when the skilled Athenian triremes outmanoeuvred and rammed the ships of the hapless Spartans and their allies. The Romans were a somewhat landlubberly race who took almost a perverse pride in their lack of nautical ability. Not for them adroit turns taking advantage of wind and current to put a trireme in a favourable position for ramming. Instead, the Romans tried to fight their naval actions in a manner as close to land combat as possible. Therefore, an ideal Roman naval battle consisted of ships drawn up alongside one another while the soldiers aboard each fought it out sword to sword.

It is quite likely that this was the sort of action the Egyptians were expecting, and indeed given the scratch nature of their fleet and the number of untrained sailors they had aboard it was quite possibly the sort of combat that they wanted. They had far greater numbers, after all.

It was left to the Rhodians to demonstrate in their minor way at sea what Caesar had convincingly shown on land in the large-scale battle of Pharsalus – that in military actions quality can generally overcome quantity. This is particularly the case where the quality – the Rhodian warship – was already suffering from considerable embarrassment for having become isolated in the first place and was viciously determined to make up for the lapse. It is also very probable that the other eleven Rhodian ships in the flotilla felt that they had their national reputation to maintain.

> In every combat the Rhodians demonstrated both excellent seamanship and great bravery. Now when battle was joined the Rhodians fought harder than ever, putting themselves in the thick of the fighting lest their fleet be defeated and they themselves be seen as the cause of it. (Ibid.)

The effect on the startled Egyptians can be imagined. They had approached in the belief that they need only approach to receive the surrender of a disorganized and demoralized crew, and instead found themselves pitted against enraged and highly-skilled opponents who fought like demons. The unskilled Egyptians were still struggling to cope with the one trireme when that trireme was no longer isolated; led by the Rhodians, the remainder of Caesar's ships had come up and fallen upon the Egyptian fleet like a pack of wolves.

The result was what the Caesarian side described as 'a highly successful action'. Two Egyptian ships were 'stripped of their marines' which can only mean that the Romans managed to kill all the hostile combatants aboard those ships before the crew successfully disengaged. One quinquereme was captured, probably by Roman legionaries rampaging from bow to stern, and substantial losses were inflicted on the combat troops aboard other vessels. Here Caesar was somewhat discombobulated by the lack of his veteran legionaries. Had he not been constrained to leave these men in Alexandria he could probably have effected more captures.

A second quinquereme was *'depressa'* – for which we should read 'sunk' although this is technically incorrect. Being made of wood, ancient warships were actually buoyancy-positive without displacement. This meant that they were quite capable of remaining afloat even after having the bottom torn out of them by a Rhodian ram, which is likely what happened in this case. However a ship so mauled was completely unseaworthy and if the wreckage could not be pulled to safety (at some risk to the rowers if the weather was bad) then the ship would be left to slowly founder on its own.

Had night not brought an end to the combat the naval side of the war might have ended right there, so completely were the Romans rolling back their confused and panicked opponents. However, Caesar was not prepared to continue fighting in the dark with his ships right against an unfamiliar shore, and by now the Egyptians were all too ready to use darkness and local knowledge to facilitate their escape from this unexpectedly bruising encounter.

As Caesar later pointed out, it was not a lack of bravery on the part of the Egyptians that led to their shattering defeat but the fact that the Roman side, with the Rhodians at the fore, had comprehensively outmanoeuvred their opponents and taken brutal advantage of that every time. In a way that was all the more demoralizing for the Egyptians, because bravery can be quickly summoned up in the right circumstances. Seamanship, on the other hand can only be taught by long experience. Therefore, no matter how speedily the Egyptian leaders restored the morale of their battered fleet, they were going to have to be able to outsail their opponents.

The Romans made sure to rub in their victory as firmly as possible. Caesar's return to Alexandria amounted to a triumphal procession through the harbour. The headwinds which had prevented the reinforcements from reaching the city in the first place had returned, but now this was less of a problem. This was because the transports largely relied upon sails, but warships of the classical era were powered by oars. Therefore, the ships of Caesar's flotilla now took the transports in tow and pulled them into harbour against the wind, which was fortunately gentle. Just as the offshore fight had demoralized the Egyptians, Caesar's legionaries would have been greatly heartened by the victorious return of their commander and the triumphant arrival of Calvinus' men and supplies.

It was always clear to the Egyptian leadership that control of the sea was vital to overall success in the war. It was now also clear that the naval situation had been somewhat mishandled in the very early stages of the crisis. After his arrival in Egypt, Caesar had been able to get his hands on the Ptolemaic fleet. At that time, no-one was contemplating that the situation would deteriorate to the point where matters now stood, and the objective of the Egyptians back then had been to encourage Caesar to leave rather than remain trapped in Egypt. Furthermore, at that time of the year most of the warships in the Great Harbour had been pulled ashore for refurbishment and the crews had been scattered around the city.

Nevertheless, with hindsight it had been a capital error not to move the navy out of Caesar's grasp in the days when Caesar had first arrived and was still feeling his way. This misstep had resulted in Caesar being able to destroy around 110 ships of various sizes, and had granted Caesar's flotilla naval control of the Great Harbour.

This realization now led to a spasm of building by the Alexandrians, for they were aware that Caesar now had both warships and transports. He could pick a target anywhere along the Alexandrian shoreline and deposit his veteran legionaries there for a raid much faster than a defensive force could be moved into place by land. Consequently barricades began springing up at vulnerable points across the city as the Alexandrians decided that the towers they had already built were rendered insufficient by Caesar's new-found mobility.

With this appreciation of the importance of sea power in the struggle, Ganymedes was determined to show that gaining control of the water late was better than never doing so. The Egyptian commander called a meeting and pointed out that Caesar had been able to obtain reinforcements and supplies only because he had the stronger fleet. This should not be allowed to happen again. Nor was the lack of ships a permanent issue. The Alexandrians were famed for their energy and industry, and they had the know-how, the will and the materials with which to construct a fresh fleet from scratch, and to construct it at record speed. Manning the fleet would be less of a problem because the sailors of the ships burned by Caesar had mostly been ashore at the time. Also, the Alexandrians as a people had been about on boats for most of their lives, and it should take minimal effort to train a navy from people already accustomed to life on the water.

Indeed, even though Caesar's flotilla controlled the waters of the Great Harbour, Alexandrians with a nautical inclination were already proving a nuisance for Caesar's men. The Alexandrians controlled the Heptastadion, the causeway linking the main city of Alexandria to the island of Pharos. They were therefore able to send small boats under the bridges of the causeway and these mounted commando raids – presumably by night – which attempted to slip across the Great Harbour and set fire to Caesar's transports. It is not known whether any of these daring attempts succeeded, but certainly they exasperated Caesar sufficiently that he took drastic steps to curtail them once the opportunity availed itself.

Someone might reasonably have asked Ganymedes why, if the Alexandrians had so many skilled sailors available, the Egyptian fleet had fared so badly against the Romans in their recent engagement. One defence would be that the news that Caesar was outside Alexandria had come as a surprise and the Egyptians had very little time to react. Therefore, the fleet which Caesar had so handily beaten up had consisted of ships crewed by whomever could be crammed aboard at short notice rather than trained sailors accustomed to working together. This would not be the case next time.

By way of an additional advantage, the royal dockyards were in Egyptian hands and plenty of timber was available. Therefore, construction of new ships should begin immediately. Furthermore, the ships that had survived the earlier naval action were to be repaired to a seaworthy condition and any older ships be located and renovated also. There were apparently a number – the exact figure is not given – of old warships mothballed in the dockyards which the Egyptians now planned to bring back into service. Another source of shipping was the guardships which patrolled the many mouths of the Delta, extracting customs duties from traders hoping to slip upriver without coming to the attention of the authorities. These guardships were now recalled to join the Egyptian fleet in Alexandria. Other ships were slowly arriving from coastal towns across the Delta, for it will be recalled that one of the last acts of the late unlamented Achillas had been to send out men to requisition whatever vessels that could be found suitable for military purposes.

In short, once Ganymedes had provided the incentive, the Egyptians threw themselves wholeheartedly into the project of raising a fresh fleet.

> In some cases, where materials were lacking, native ingenuity countered the deficit. In other cases the want was met from the city's resources. (*Alexandrine War* 13)

One example of this was demonstrated when it was discovered that the mothballed warships did not have any oars. (New warships required fresh hulls, but the oars could be readily transferred from older ships to the new, so the city's supply of oars had burned up with the ships destroyed in the harbour.)

However, all that was needed for fresh oars was a good supply of long, straight timber, so the Alexandrians set about dismantling public buildings, colonnades and any structure large enough to have long beams of wood holding up a roof. Once resolved upon that sacrifice, the Alexandrians were able to produce oars as fast as the city's carpenters could churn them out. Quantity rather than quality was in demand, since most of the ships being brought so hastily into service were for short-term use. They would never operate outside the harbour of Alexandria and need not be built to withstand the rigours of a long sea voyage.

Their early experience with the Alexandrians had evoked from the Romans reluctant admiration of their energy and ability. Even so, it must have come as a considerable shock to Caesar's men when – within a matter of days – they saw a new fleet being prepared for sea trials in the harbour. In quinqueremes and triremes the new Egyptian vessels outnumbered the warships of Caesar's fleet twenty-seven to ten, and the odds were considerably greater when it came to smaller undecked boats. It seemed that rather than permanently crippling the Egyptians' naval capabilities, Caesar had merely handed them a setback. Now he had to do it all over again.

Working on the principle that it was better to deal with the Egyptian fleet before the enemy sailors had become accustomed to their new ships, their commanders and each other, Caesar immediately ordered his flotilla to take on this new enemy. Once again he was betting the superior skill of his veterans against the greater number of his enemy.

Chapter 8

The Battle for Eunostos Harbour

At this point it is worth revisiting the geography of Alexandria's harbour [based largely on Belov, A., *Navigational aspects of calling to the Great Harbour of Alexandria*, Center for Egyptological Studies of the Russian Academy of Sciences, 2014]. This port was close to being two entirely separate harbours, the Great Harbour to the northeast, and the Eunostos Harbour to the southwest. Today this division is an established fact because the shoreline of Alexandria has changed considerably over the centuries. While the modern city has the harbours divided by a ridge of land that makes the former island of Pharos now firmly a part of the mainland, in Caesar's time this division was artificial and what is now a ridge of land was then the long artificial causeway of the Heptastadion, which in some places was actually a bridge beneath which small craft could sail.

The bridges and canals were deliberately cut through the causeway to allow for the easy transfer of ships from one harbour to the another. The reason for this 'double port' was because the prevailing winds blow from two directions – northeast and southwest, and even in the most violent of storms at least one harbour was completely sheltered, and vulnerable ships would be moved accordingly.

The Great Harbour in the northeast was controlled by Caesar's flotilla. The most northerly arm of the harbour was the Lachias Promontory which was extended by an artificial seawall to a small islet which marked the most northerly point of the city. This islet was situated around a hundred metres from the most northeasterly point of the island of Pharos, creating a restricted entrance (the Alveus

Steganus or 'hidden channel') to the Great Harbour which allowed better control of both shipping and offshore waves.

Opposite the islet was the Great Lighthouse, both a symbol of the power of Ptolemaic Egypt and a highly necessary structure, for very little of the Egyptian coastline at this point is very high above the waves. Without assistance from the lighthouse, ancient sailors might only know that they had struck land when they did so literally on one of the many local reefs and sandbanks. (These sandbanks were also a problem for sailors entering the southwestern Eunostos Harbour, for several sandbars lay right across the harbour mouth.)

The island of Pharos was just over a kilometre offshore, a twisting spit of land less than half a kilometre at the widest and less than a hundred metres wide at the point where the Lighthouse – as tall as a modern skyscraper – towered over the city. This small spit of land, about 800 metres long and around 1.5 kilometres from where the Heptastadion joined the island, was all that Caesar currently controlled, but as this gave him control of the entrance to the Great Harbour, it was all the control that he had needed until now. (In later years the spit linking the lighthouse to the rest of Pharos Island was washed away altogether leaving the lighthouse isolated.)

It seems probable from the description of events in the *Alexandrine War* that the revitalized Egyptian fleet was located in the Eunostos Harbour so that the sailors could run through their first practice drills without interference from Caesar's fleet. Because of the sandbars at the entrance, there were two possible routes into Eunostos – the Poseidon Channel alongside the island of Pharos, and the Bull Channel on the Alexandrian side. From there one had to cross the whole harbour to reach the Kibotus quay where the Egyptian ships were probably docked against the Heptastadion. (The Alexandrian quays were very solid affairs of stone and concrete held together with bronze clamps, and so substantial that they are still largely in position today, although either buried beneath the modern shoreline, or submerged completely offshore.)

Therefore, to get at the newly raised Egyptian fleet, Caesar had to leave the Great Harbour, sail out into the open sea, around Pharos Island and then into Eunostos Harbour – which is what he did. The Egyptians observed his progress with interest, and with plenty of time to deploy. They drew up their fleet in the centre of the harbour with twenty-two of their strongest ships at the centre of their battleline and the others behind in reserve. Around these swarmed a host of smaller craft that hoped to overwhelm Caesar's fleet with sheer numbers.

The main weapons on the smaller boats were flaming torches. An ancient warship was largely dried timber caulked with pitch, and fire was a constant hazard, even if without rigging and a large linen sail (the sails were usually dismounted and left ashore when a planned naval confrontation was imminent).

As he approached the harbour, Caesar put his elite Rhodian ships on the right, Pharos Island side where the Poseidon Channel controlled movement in and out of the harbour, and his Pontic ships were positioned 400 metres to the left, facing the Bull Channel. Then with the two fleets facing each other a stand-off ensued. Between the antagonists lay the sandbars that, apart from the two channels, barred entrance to the harbour. A fleet entering or exiting Eunostos had necessarily to pass through one of these channels, which made it vulnerable as the ships entered one by one.

Furthermore, even if a fleet could successfully pass through the channels and redeploy, if it were defeated it would have to leave the battle via that same bottleneck, doubtless taking heavy casualties all the while. So the battle began with a game of chicken, with the fleets on opposite sides of the entrance, each daring the other to come over to their side and engage. As the aggressor, the first move was up to Caesar for it quickly became clear that the Alexandrians had no intention of coming out to fight. All the Alexandrians had to do was wait and if Caesar declined to enter Eunostos their sailors could row back to their quay. They could have then crossed the Heptastadion to jeer at Caesar's flotilla as it made a humiliating return around Pharos Island after a pointless excursion.

Therefore Caesar had a choice. He could pull back or he could order his men to fight their way into Eunostos, with the first ships into the harbour taking the brunt of the Egyptian attack while the rest of the fleet formed up behind them. For this difficult and dangerous approach to succeed those first ships would require crews both skilled and fearless. In short, Caesar would need the Rhodians. With casual racism the writer of the *Alexandrine War* describes the commander of the Rhodian ships as one 'Euphranor, a man who in terms of his personality and courage is more like one of our own [Roman] people than a Greek'.

By this account it was the Rhodians who approached Caesar and requested that they be allowed to serve as the spearhead of the Roman attack. Caesar heaped praise upon Euphranor and his men and prepared the rest of his flotilla to follow their lead. The Rhodians sent in four ships – which number was presumably all that could travel down the channel in line of battle. The Alexandrians advanced their fleet to meet the intruders and the Rhodians plunged into the midst of the enemy.

It may be imagined that matters were highly confused for several minutes thereafter. The Alexandrians had on their side numbers and enthusiasm. The Rhodians had cold competence, and to a counter-intuitive degree, also an advantage in their small number. That is, a swarm of badly-trained amateur sailors could not prevent their own ships from getting in one another's way, and the need to avoid their small boats prevented the quinqueremes and triremes from getting into the positions they needed for a ram or a sweep. To ram an opponent, an ancient warship had to hit its opponent broadside on at speed. However, the sheer enthusiasm of the smaller craft attacking the Rhodians prevented the Egyptian warships from getting a clear run at their target.

The alternative was to attempt a sweep, which was when a large ship came unexpectedly alongside an enemy, again while moving at speed. The attacker needed to have time for its own crew to ship their oars. Then, if the men on the opposing ship failed to do the same promptly enough, the attacker would plough through the banks of oars still in the water, sweeping some away, snapping others and causing chaos among the rowers on the other end. A successful sweep left a ship without oars on one side and the rowers often injured or incapacitated. With their ship only able to move in a slow circle the victims of a successful sweep were sitting ducks for a follow-up attack – and usually this attack featured a ram.

It must have been frustrating for the Alexandrian captains to have the advantage of overwhelming numbers and yet not be able to land a single telling blow upon their nimble opponents. The Rhodians handled their four ships as a single unit, while the Alexandrians could not do the same because it was for precisely that reason they had been out in the harbour getting much-needed practice in the first place. Eventually the masterclass in hard experience taught by the Rhodian four came to an end because the remaining Rhodian triremes had joined the battle with the rest of Caesar's ships piling in behind them.

At this point the waters just inside the harbour became such a tangled mass of ships and fighting men that skilled manoeuvres were impossible. It now came down to close combat between the ships jammed together alongside one another. The Alexandrians had the edge because they were fighting in home waters. Not only did they know the harbour intimately, they had friends and family cheering them on from roofs of houses all along the shore on the Pharos side. There were others on the Alexandrian shore, but the people there could offer only moral support. Those on the Pharos side could do better, because any time one of their ships was getting worsted in combat the crew needed only move closer to the Pharos shore.

At this point those on the rooftops ceased to be merely passive spectators and actively joined the combat by showering any Roman vessel which dared follow up a retreating enemy with a hail of bricks, roof-tiles and any more formal weaponry such as spears that those on the rooftops had been able to grab at short notice. The Egyptian ship which had moved under cover of this impromptu artillery barrage could then offload its wounded, take aboard fresh combatants and charge once more into the fray.

On the other hand, the Romans had no such advantage. Any of their ships locked in combat had to fight or die where it was, since moving shoreward increased its peril even as it tilted the odds in favour of its Alexandrian opponent. The same issue of a handy sanctuary in combat applied to the Roman and Alexandrian fleets as a whole. If they decided that they were getting the worse of the combat the Alexandrian leaders could signal the fleet to break off and retreat to near the Heptastadion, where the Egyptian shore artillery – possibly including some of their mobile towers – could protect their ships at the quay.

If the Romans were forced to retreat they would have to do as they had when advancing – get through the Poseidon Channel four at a time with the Egyptians now relentlessly attacking their rearguard. Caesar was aware of this – in fact he had not only understood this from the beginning but had taken the time to explain to his men the problem that they would be facing. In short, the Romans had walked with eyes wide open into the trap, fully confident of their ability to fight their way out of it again.

It also helped greatly that Caesar now had his veteran soldiers aboard his ships, and ships jammed close together created something of a semblance of a land battle. The author of the *Alexandrine War* stresses that the deciding factor was the greater bravery of the Romans, and their knowledge that each man could implicitly rely upon those fighting alongside him. These were veteran troops accustomed to the grim business of killing and having others try to kill them – a situation which generally disconcerts those such as the Alexandrians who were in it for the first time. It also helped Caesar that the Alexandrians knew that they could call off the fight at any time while the Romans simply had to win, and fought all the harder for that reason.

These factors led to an Alexandrian quinquereme surrendering, and then a bireme also fell into Roman hands complete with rowers and combat crew. This may have decided the remainder of the Alexandrian fleet to call it a day and retreat back to the docks. At some point a further three Alexandrian vessels were 'sunk', and this probably occurred as the retreating Alexandrian ships left the Rhodians with open water in which to do what they did best – which was to manoeuvre around their unskilled opponents and hit them amidships.

> The remainder of their ships retreated to the shore and the protection of the townsfolk who had taken up positions on the Heptastadion and nearby buildings. From there they were able to prevent our men from continuing the engagement.
> (*Alexandrine War* 16)

At this point one may legitimately wonder why Caesar had bothered engaging in this battle at all. Apart from giving his men healthy exercise and a day on the water away from the Lachias Peninsula there would seem to have been little that he could achieve, and a great deal that he stood to lose. After all, the Alexandrians could break off from combat any time they wanted, or indeed could have refused to fight at all. On the other hand, had the fortunes of war not favoured Caesar then he and his flotilla might have finished their war right there at the bottom of the unfriendly waters of Eunostos Harbour.

Therefore we must assume that Caesar's intention in making this high-risk move was never to defeat the Alexandrian fleet – it was to gain control of the harbour. Once he had secured the Eunostos Harbour and could put ships right alongside the Heptastadion, Caesar could prevent the Egyptians from sending reinforcements to the garrison on his main objective – the island of Pharos.

Pharos was strategically important to the battle for Alexandria for several reasons. Caesar already held the most important bit of the island – the northeast tip which contained the Lighthouse. This meant that the Romans commanded access to the Great Harbour and could – as Caesar had just demonstrated – move in and out at will. An under-estimated bonus of control of the Lighthouse was that it was by far the tallest building in Alexandria. In fact, at the height of a modern skyscraper, the Lighthouse was at that time pretty much the tallest building anywhere. (To count as a skyscraper a building must be at least 100 metres high. The Lighthouse was at least 110 metres.)

This height meant that the Lighthouse could be seen far out to sea. It also meant that those atop the Lighthouse could see just as far in the other direction. Given that most of Alexandria and the surrounding countryside of the Nile delta was extremely low-lying, the Lighthouse gave Caesar an unparalleled view of what his opponents were up to in Alexandria, the Eunostos Harbour and the countryside beyond.

Useful as the northeast tip of Pharos was to Caesar, he now wanted control of the whole island. This was because the island made up the seaward shore of Eunostos Harbour. When Caesar's flotilla had forced its way into the harbour it was completely in enemy territory, while Alexandrian ships in trouble had only to retreat towards the shore – any shore – to be safe. Now Caesar coveted that same protection for his fleet within the hostile harbour.

Attacking the city side of the harbour was impractical because the enemy could easily bring up reinforcements, and the Romans would have to fight continually on a relatively wide front to defend their gains. However, if Caesar could gain control of Pharos then an attack on his forces holding the Pharos shore could only come by sea – with the Romans holding the all-important advantage of height atop the rooftops and towers abutting the harbour along the Heptastadion causeway. And a bridge, as the Roman Horatius had demonstrated hundred of years previously, was eminently defensible.

Yet, if Pharos could be held with relative ease once it was in Roman hands, the same factors that would prevent the Alexandrians from retaking the island were factors that made it difficult for Caesar to capture Pharos in the first place. The first obstacle, of course, had been that the Alexandrians controlled the waters of Eunostos Harbour, and therefore sea access to much of the island's shoreline. This control the Alexandrians no longer had and getting that control marked Caesar's first step in getting control of Pharos Island.

So now, with the enemy fleet driven back to the quay on the Alexandrian side, the Roman assault on Pharos began. The first attack was made on defences on the city side of the harbour. This was not because Caesar had any interest at this time in securing the docks there, but because it distracted the Alexandrians. While they hurried to fight off the attack nearest their homes, they paid little attention to those ships of Caesar's flotilla which slipped out of Eunostos and sailed out of sight to the seaward side of Pharos.

These were Caesar's heavy ships – the triremes and quinqueremes – which looked most formidable. Their job was to open another front and make it look as though the main attack on Pharos was to come from the seaward side. Though this was mainly to draw away defenders from the harbour side of Pharos, Caesar was well aware that if the defenders of the island were caught off-guard this attack might actually succeed, and he had accordingly offered substantial rewards to any of his men who succeeded in establishing a bridgehead there. Certainly, this was no trivial feint – Caesar had allocated most of a legion and his light troops and cavalry to this attack.

There is no information as to what was happening among the troops who were already holding the spit of land which included the Great Lighthouse, but given that Caesar wanted to create maximum confusion among the island's defenders so as to disguise his true point of attack, it would be surprising if the troops guarding the Lighthouse had not also been instructed to make aggressive moves.

The true point of attack was the Eunostos Harbour side of Pharos. This place already had quays and a harbour for Caesar's troop-laden ships to dock and was anyway the part of the island that Caesar most needed to take. Once he had somewhere to park his ships in Eunostos Harbour, Caesar could take the rest of Pharos at his leisure. Once the attack was launched, it quickly became clear that the defenders of Pharos had no intention of making things easy for Caesar's men. Nor did the physical layout of the harbour help. Access to those tempting quays where Caesar wanted to offload his legionaries was restricted, and the narrow waterways were guarded by harbour pinnaces, and also by five full-scale warships – which had probably retreated in that direction once the fight in the open harbour had started to go against them. Annoyingly, the harbour pinnaces were speedy enough to outmanoeuvre Caesar's sea-going ships, and the warships were among those enemy ships which happened to have skilled crews.

Other elements of Caesar's army attempted to storm the beaches not occupied by port facilities. The problem here was that there was a reason that these beaches were not used by shipping – the shoreline was not really suited for that purpose, which meant that it was also not ideal for an amphibious assault. When it came to defending these beaches the Alexandrians on Pharos were not only prepared to use their rooftops as launch points for light artillery, they were prepared to come down to the beaches and engage with the Romans hand-to-hand as they struggled out of the water.

Yet those men attempting to fight their way ashore were not the enthusiastic-but-somewhat-unskilled militias who made up the citizen contingent of the Egyptian army, or even the trained veterans of the renegade Gabinian legions. These were the battle-hardened elite of Caesar's Legio VI – already severely diminished by attrition in combat in lands right across the Mediterranean, but composed now of men both extremely experienced at not dying and at making their opponents do so. Once these veteran soldiers had found a way across the difficult terrain of the shallows and obtained a toehold on dry land, they took up battle formation and began to chop their way through the opposition.

In fact, once the Sixth had formed a battleline across the foreshore the fight was over in practical terms. The only question was whether the Alexandrian defenders would stand their ground and get chopped to pieces or run as soon as the legionaries launched their charge. Sensibly, they selected option two, and fled to the cover of the buildings. This allowed the legionaries to move along the shore and approach the docks from the side where they were relatively undefended. Once the men aboard the Egyptian ships defending the quays realized that the docks behind them were falling into Roman hands, they had to abandon their positions or be surrounded. Accordingly, they backed up their ships to the built-up area by the waterfront and disembarked to continue the fight from the buildings.

These buildings had great potential for defence. They were built side-by-side to the point where they formed an almost continuous line rather like a city wall which averaged some thirty feet high. This presented a serious obstacle to Roman legionaries who had attacked from ships and were therefore short of the usual facilities required for such an assault. Scaling ladders would have been useful, and also the large wicker shields that the Romans habitually used to protect those conducting operations within missile range. In short, the Romans now held the docks on Pharos, but getting inland looked as though it would present a serious challenge to Caesar's already weary legionaries.

That challenge did not materialize. If Caesar's troops had just had a tough day, it had been even harder for the Alexandrians who had just seen their fleet defeated, despite their ships having the superior tactical position, and the harbour facilities taken by Roman legionaries, despite the defenders holding every advantage. Under the circumstances it was understandable that they were less than firm in their belief that they could hold the buildings of the shoreline against Caesar's apparently unstoppable forces. Many of those who had been confident they could hold off Caesar's legionaries on the level ground of the beach remained on that beach as bloody corpses – a grim reminder that trying to hold off the Roman attack came with lethal consequences.

A few enterprising souls decided that for themselves personally the best solution lay not in fighting grimly to defend the buildings but to take a running dive into the harbour and swim the 800 metres or so to the city side. Once these first swimmers had reached sanctuary, others followed, and every deserting defender lowered the morale of those remaining. To conquer those apparently unassailable walls it seemed that all the legionaries had to do was stand about and look menacing while the defence crumbled before their eyes. When the barricades were sufficiently depleted, the legionaries went through the formality of storming the buildings and once the remaining defenders on the island saw that the shoreline was lost the surrenders accelerated.

It is not known how many of the Alexandrians who took to the water were captured and killed by the Romans in their boats, but some 6,000 prisoners in all were taken during this phase of the operation. As a reward for what had been a difficult day so far, Caesar gave his men permission to plunder the buildings, and afterwards ordered that they be demolished. It is significant that Caesar ordered the destruction of buildings which formed a useful line of defence along the Pharos shoreline. His orders suggest that he was not confident of holding that part of the island and did not want to have to go to the same degree of effort if he ever needed to attack there again – especially if the defenders did their job somewhat better the second time around.

For the present, the next item on Caesar's somewhat crowded agenda was the Heptastadion. His warships now held the Eunostos and Great harbours, but Pharos would not be safely in his hands if the enemy could still mount an attack along the causeway. The flight of the defenders of Pharos had included those who defended the first of the bridges which allowed ships to pass from one harbour to the other. This bridge was now taken and barricaded by Caesar's legions.

Thus there was already a cork in that particular bottle, but Caesar wanted control of most of the causeway, presumably because this would allow him to transfer elements of his fleet from one harbour to the other without the need to sail around Pharos. Equally importantly it would prevent the Alexandrians and their annoying fleets of small boats from slipping under the bridge for their nightly attempts at sabotage.

However, the second bridge on the Heptastadion was situated very close to the Alexandrian shore and was still in Alexandrian hands. Being narrow, it was easily defended and was also well within missile range of the shore, so overall Caesar decided that it seemed best to leave things as they were and call it a day. After all, the Romans had taken Pharos and now dominated both harbours of Alexandria. The rest of the causeway could wait until the morrow. Nevertheless, Caesar was determined to take the bridges and end 'the sallies and sudden forays of enemy boats' which had been making life difficult for the crews of Roman ships at anchor in the Great Harbour.

The next morning demonstrated why Roman control of the waters of both harbours became useful. The narrow bridge could easily be held by a few defenders. It has been pointed out that the Roman Horatius had set the standard for holding bridges against overwhelming odds a few centuries previously. However, when holding off the Etruscan horde Horatius and friends had only to defend against attackers on the bridge itself. There were no warships laden with bowmen and artillery sailing up alongside to empty cargoes of missiles into their midst. Under attack by infantry from the front and by naval artillery on both sides the defenders reluctantly abandoned their barricade to three cohorts of legionaries which Caesar put ashore to hold his new capture.

While a rampart was being hastily thrown up on the townward side of the bridge, more ships came from Pharos Island laden with rubble. (Plenty was available since the demolishing of the houses on the Pharos shoreline had now begun.) This rubble was packed into the space beneath the town-side bridge, ensuring that it would take a major engineering effort before the passage between the harbours was once more navigable.

Again we see here a lack of belief on the Roman side that it would be possible to hold on to all that had been gained in the past two days. Caesar would doubtless prefer to have both bridges available for his ships to pass under, and the fact that he ordered the blocking of a passage already under his control speaks to a lack of belief that he could keep it that way. The reasons for that lack of belief were already rallying on the Alexandrian side. The people of Alexandria had seen their fleet defeated, Pharos captured and the Heptastadion fall into Caesar's hands. They were furious and planning to do something about it.

There was a mole extending into the harbour, parallel to the Heptastadion, where many of the Alexandrian ships had docked after their unsuccessful defence of Eunostos Harbour the previous day. The Romans seem to have been able to partly occupy this during their attack on the bridge. According to Caesar, this occupation was unplanned – rowers aboard his warships and some of the soldiers decided to disembark and watch the attack on the bridge from this advantageous viewpoint, and others were inspired by a desire to get more closely involved in the fighting. Using slings and stones they attacked the crews of the ships anchored on the mole and forced the ships to cast anchor.

There is something about this story as fishy as the denizens of the waters beside the mole. Firstly, if the mole afforded a good view of the bridge and the ships attacking alongside, then Caesar would certainly want to take that position if only to save his men from either a flank attack or enfilading fire. In other words, if he did not order men on to the mole, he should have done. However, the Romans who had disembarked on to the mole were light troops and poorly organized – either because this was indeed an ad hoc occupation, or because Caesar was not expecting trouble on that front and was taken by surprise when the Alexandrians counter-attacked.

(One notes that according to Caesar, all his operations throughout his wars were perfectly co-ordinated and successful. When something did come unstuck, this was invariably the fault of over-enthusiastic subordinates acting alone and without orders. So it comes as no surprise that when describing the unsuccessful occupation of the mole Caesar is careful to point out that he was completely innocent of ordering that occupation in the first place.)

The problem was the ships which Caesar's light infantry had driven off the mole. These ships had to go somewhere, and they chose a spot slightly further to the south. This put them on the flank of the light infantry who by now would have already been engaging with the Alexandrians to their front. Unhappy about having enemies on two sides, the light infantry began to fall back toward Caesar's ships which still occupied the waters between the mole and the Heptastadion. The sight of the Romans in retreat encouraged others on the Alexandrian ships to disembark and join in the attack on the mole, and this in turn encouraged the Caesarian troops to retreat faster.

The collapse of the flank meant that the troops manning the front against the general population of Alexandria also had to back off and a somewhat chaotic retreat started to evolve into something nearer a rout. It did not help that the Roman ships that had unloaded the light infantry on to the mole noted the deteriorating situation there. They began to ship their gang-planks preparatory to moving away from the mole lest they either be swamped by panicked troops swarming aboard, or even overwhelmed should a sudden rush of Alexandrians catch them before they could push off.

Having chaos suddenly erupt on their right affected the legionaries holding the bridge. They were already under sustained attack from the townsfolk on their front as they attempted to strengthen the rampart blocking the Heptastadion off from the town. Now they saw their support ships wavering and pushing off for the open waters of the harbour, and discovered that they were vulnerable to missile fire on their flank – and worse than missile fire if the Alexandrians should take to small boats and cross the gap between the bridge and the mole. Indeed, it seems as though some Alexandrians had already done just that and were on the Heptastadion behind them.

Caesar's attack was rapidly coming unravelled. There was a chaotic situation on the mole and the infantry on the bridge were uncertain whether to stand their ground, retreat or disembark on to the nearby warships before those ships departed. It was the departing ships which were the decisive factor. Fearing that they would be surrounded and abandoned to the untender mercies of the Alexandrians, the infantry rushed the nearest ships, desperate to get aboard before the ships left their anchorage. So many crowded aboard that at least one ship foundered under their weight. This made the other ships all the keener to push off, and panicked even further those who saw their only chance of safety about to be closed off.

A forlorn attempt by some brave souls to muster some form of rearguard was quickly overwhelmed by the Alexandrians who were storming forward, encouraged by the prospect of a rare victory. The deaths of the men in the rearguard did little to encourage the fighting spirit of the others, and certainly discouraged any thought of surrender. A few strong swimmers dove into the water and swam for the ships, but this was no easy feat for men encumbered with 10kg or more of mail armour. The swimmers task was made even harder because they had to swim while holding their shields above their heads as the Alexandrians bombarded these floating targets with whatever missiles were available.

Caesar was in no way lacking in physical courage, and he had rushed to the scene as soon as he saw that the defence of the bridge was collapsing. Yet there was little that even his tactical genius could do to retrieve the situation. The mole was lost, along with whatever rowers and light infantry had not managed to gain safety aboard the ships. The legionaries on the bridge had a mob of baying Alexandrians at their backs and were probably now taking fire from the mole. Even had his troops been willing to listen to orders, by now the situation had so deteriorated that the only practical order to give would have been 'retreat' and this Caesar's soldiers were already doing as fast as they were able.

The sudden switch from a coordinated Roman attack to a calamitous retreat shows again the fickle nature of warfare in the ancient world and why commanders of all stripes spent so much time and effort in exhorting gods and men before battle. In a situation where combat was mainly hand-to-hand everything depended upon men who were necessarily deprived of situational information beyond their immediate locality. Yet those same men were well aware that their very lives depended on what was happening elsewhere. The result was that even the best units were liable to sudden panics, and once panic developed it was highly contagious. It was a brutal fact of ancient warfare that when a battleline collapsed it was the bravest who died first. The best chance of survival lay with those who departed early and at speed – the very people in fact who were now safely aboard the Roman warships on Eunostos Harbour watching the travails of those who had remained to fight a bit longer.

Realizing that the situation was untenable, Caesar withdrew to his own vessel. Those around Caesar saw their commander retiring from the fray and drew the correct conclusion that they were doomed unless they accompanied him. So many began shoving aboard Caesar's boat that he quickly worked out what was about to happen, and anticipated the disaster by pulling off his purple general's cloak and jumping over the side before his ship capsized. While Caesar escaped into the water his distinctive cloak was recognized and gleefully captured by the Alexandrians who treated it as a battle trophy. (The incident is described in detail by Appian, *Civil Wars* 2.13.90.)

We do not know if Caesar was wearing armour upon this occasion, but in any case he was a strong swimmer. Suetonius reports (*Life of Caesar* 57) that when in a hurry Caesar would swim across any rivers between him and his army, 'often arriving before the messengers sent to announce his arrival'. Nor should Caesar's aquatic ability be a great surprise – Romans were fond of a dip in the Tiber, and many Roman men and women were expert swimmers. The writer of the *Alexandrine War* does not add a detail – or embellishment – supplied by Plutarch, namely that Caesar had important papers with him.

> So he threw himself into the sea and escaped by swimming. This was particularly difficult because he was holding a sheaf of papers in his hand. He did not want to let go of these, so while he was in the water with missiles flying at him he held them clear with one hand and swam with the other.
>
> (Plutarch, *Caesar* 49,8)

Once Caesar had swum to a ship further offshore, he gave orders that the harbour pinnaces captured at Pharos should be used to embark those legionaries still trapped on the Heptastadion. The rest of the day is evidently something that Caesar did not really want to talk about, although he admits to losing around 800 to 1,000 men. Some 400 of these were legionaries, and as we know that three cohorts were deployed for this action (p.105) it would appear that casualties were at least 30 per cent of the force on the Heptastadion. In fact, if these were legionaries of Caesar's Sixth, the casualty rate was even higher because we know that legion was severely under strength. The remaining casualties were rowers and light infantry – painful in itself, but nowhere as crippling as the loss of irreplaceable legionaries.

Certainly the Heptastadion was lost, and even more frustratingly the second bridge was lost before the arch could be completely blocked with rubble. With their usual energy, the Alexandrians promptly set about clearing the debris, and at the same time they reinforced the rampart begun by Caesar's soldiers. Just to make sure that the Romans could not once again bring their ships alongside this rampart, they added artillery support both on the Heptastadion and within range on the mainland.

It is unknown if Caesar managed to hold his gains on Pharos Island, although the fact that the Romans destroyed the beachfront houses when they had a chance is significant. This tells us that they were more concerned with slighting the island's defences than they were about using these defences to hold off an Alexandrian attack. In other words, while it would be nice if the Romans could hold on to Pharos permanently, Caesar was well aware that this was probably not going to happen. Even with his reinforcements he was stretched for manpower and after the debacle on the Heptastadion even more so. In the face of an Alexandrian attack along the Heptastadion he could use his control of the waters of the harbour to evacuate the men on Pharos to safety, and with the defences crippled it would be easier for the Romans to re-take the island when they needed control of Eunostos Harbour.

As it turned out, Caesar had no need to take the whole of Pharos. He certainly needed the part that controlled the Lighthouse and the entrance to the Great Harbour, but in the end the rest of the island turned out to be militarily irrelevant. So, the question becomes why did Caesar expend so much time and blood on an objective that played no part in the later campaign?

The answer tells us something about Caesar the general. He was what modern management theory would call a 'systems' man rather than an 'objectives' one. An 'objectives' general would be one who formulates a plan and then proceeds step by step through its execution until either success or some form of derailment takes place, in which case a fresh plan is required. A 'systems' general hardly has a plan at all, but instead attempts to adjust prevailing circumstances to his advantage so that eventually he will get an opportunity to strike a decisive blow.

The Duke of Wellington was a systems man who later remarked that the French made plans that resembled an elaborate horse's bridle.

Elegant and effective, but useless should the thing break. Wellington's bridle, he claimed, was like a length of rope, which he could simply knot at the break and carry on.

So it was with Caesar at Pharos. When he attempted to take the entire island, Caesar probably had no idea what he was going to do with it – and indeed he had a pretty-clear inkling that he was not going to be able to hang on to it. However, it was also clear to him that Pharos Island in his hands was better than Pharos Island in Egyptian hands, so he might as well go for it. With the uncertainties of war, it may turn out that possession of the island was vital for some reason, and Caesar would bitterly regret not having seized it when he had the chance. In the end, possession of the island turned out not to matter. But this does not mean that Caesar was wrong to want to have it under his control when the chance presented itself.

For the present though, it seems that the situation returned to how it had been before Caesar launched his breakout attack on the Alexandrian fleet. The Romans retreated to the royal palaces on the Lachias Peninsula and doubtless kept a firm grip on the promontory holding the Pharos lighthouse. The Egyptians returned to scheming how they were going to get Caesar out of there. They knew that Caesar had only to wait until the rest of Rome's armies got word that their commander was in trouble and came to his rescue. Time was not on the Egyptian side.

Chapter 9

A Change of Management

If there was for Caesar a silver lining to the debacle on the Heptastadion, it was the way that his legionaries reacted to the setback. The battle-hardened veterans of his key legion, the Sixth, were furious. Legio VI Hispaniensis had rallied around Caesar at the moment when the Gauls looked like breaking the Roman siege of Alesia which ended the Gallic Wars. Then the legion had fought against Republican armies in Spain and had gone through the tribulations of the Greek campaign to help Caesar win the Battle of Pharsalus, the victory which made their commander master of the Roman world. The Sixth had a lot to be proud of, and its soldiers set the standard to which the new recruits of the Twenty-eighth Legion aspired. For such men, imbued with both regimental and nationalist pride, it was intolerable and insulting that they had been comprehensively beaten by the Alexandrians – a mixed mob of retired soldiers and civilians who were not even Romans.

Fortunately for the legionaries they did not have to look far for targets upon which to vent their fury. Inspired by victory, the Alexandrians went on the offensive and tried to retake Roman positions on the Lachias Peninsula with large-scale sallies. These ran into ferocious resistance and several major street battles resulted. How the battles turned out can be inferred from the fact that thereafter the Romans set about counter-attacking Alexandrian redoubts and achieving considerable success as they did so. In the end Caesar had to tell his men to curb their enthusiasm because he could neither afford to lose more men nor take new ground – he had barely the manpower to hold on to what he had already.

This Roman bloodthirstiness seems to have rather nonplussed the Alexandrians. Caesar's men had proven themselves to be such vicious and experienced fighters that overwhelming them by sheer numbers was clearly not going to work. On the other hand, it also seemed unlikely that the legionaries were going to do what any rational Hellenistic unit would have done under those circumstances, which was to turn over their commander to the enemy and join the winning side. In fact, according to the author of the *Alexandrine War*, the Alexandrians now found it difficult to see what was going to demoralize an enemy who was fired up by setbacks and heartened by success.

At this point it is even more unfortunate that the later historian of events has to rely upon a far-from-impartial source for an account of what the Alexandrians were thinking. After all, a fervently pro-Caesar writer who refers to the Alexandrians as 'a deceitful breed, always lying to hide their real intentions' is hardly going to give an unbiased account of their deliberations, yet regrettably that account is all that we have to go on. So we do not really know why at this point the Egyptians called for a truce. Indeed, the writer of the *Alexandrine War* frankly admits that he also does not know why the Egyptians did so.

Logically speaking, it was reasonable enough to call for a ceasefire because there was no particular reason why the war should have broken out in the first place. After all, the Romans had intervened in the matter of the Ptolemaic kingship on previous occasions without it leading to the present degree of bloodshed, and in this case Caesar was only enforcing the terms specified in the will of the previous Pharaoh. In fact, this wholly avoidable and unnecessary war had been brought about by unscrupulous power-hungry officials on the Egyptian side and a lamentable lack of diplomacy on Caesar's part.

It may be that some sensible souls on the Alexandrian side took a step back and decided that the current situation presented an ideal opportunity to make peace. The Alexandrians had been infuriated from the start by Caesar's high-handed approach but now, after their success on the Heptastadion, it could be argued that Caesar had been made to pay for his arrogance. At the same time, the reaction of the legionaries to their setback served as a warning to the Alexandrians not to push their luck.

At present Caesar's men had their backs to the wall, and while they were very good at fighting from that position, they were certainly more likely to be amenable to reason than they would be once reinforcements arrived from the rest of the Roman world, as was certain to happen sooner or later. If ever there was a moment for both sides to call it a draw and negotiate a peace, this was it.

Caesar had little to lose from negotiations, or indeed from a peace settlement. Every day without fighting was a day in which he did not lose any more men before the arrival of help from abroad. Even if the terms of a settlement turned out to be less than satisfactory in the short term, renegotiations would be possible in the future should Caesar return with his Sixth Legion, and also the Fifth, Seventh, Eighth, Ninth and Tenth legions.

In fact the Egyptians were probably aware that further troops were already on the way to reinforce Caesar's beleaguered garrison. There was a large body of men advancing by land from Syria, and a smaller advance guard sent ahead by sea – the intention probably being to give Caesar's men some extra heft to help them to hold out until the main relief force arrived. The Alexandrians hoped (probably in vain) that Caesar was as yet unaware of these impending arrivals and might have to negotiate from a perceived position of relative weakness.

The main obstacle to peace was the leadership on the Egyptian side. Arsinoe was well aware that her only path to the Egyptian throne ran over Caesar's body. Any political settlement was bound to see Ptolemy XIII as pharaoh, or Cleopatra, or both. In any of these cases, the future for Arsinoe was likely to be bleak and short. The Ptolemies tended to be very abrupt with family members who were a threat to their position, and Arsinoe had proven herself to be a very serious threat indeed.

Yet, if the Alexandrians did succeed in killing Caesar, then his rebellion against the Roman Republic might well fall apart, since Caesar had no obvious successor. The Republican cause had already rallied in Africa and Spain and, with Caesar gone, Italy might next return to Republican rule. Under such circumstances Arsinoe would be a hero to the Alexandrian people and a firm friend of the resurgent Roman Republic. Once that happened, both Cleopatra and Ptolemy would be doomed and Arsinoe would be undisputed ruler of Egypt. She had every reason to keep fighting, and her general Ganymedes was her creature who would stand and fall with her.

Given these circumstances, it was very reasonable that an Alexandrian peace party – if indeed one such did exist – would conclude that the best way to resolve this unnecessary fracas was to replace the current Egyptian leadership with someone more suitable. And someone more suitable was available. Young Ptolemy XIII had been pharaoh of Egypt before, and no-one on the Alexandrian side (apart from Arsinoe) would object if he were to be pharaoh once again. Given that the Egyptian palace had been riddled with intrigue long before the arrival of the Romans it is certain that lines of communication were open across the battlefront between the palace and city of Alexandria.

Reports from the palace would have informed the Alexandrians that relationships between Caesar and young Ptolemy had improved considerably. Caesar could be extremely charming when he put his mind to it, and Cleopatra was certainly no slouch at diplomacy on a personal level. Between the two of them they seemed to have wheedled Ptolemy around – a task made all the easier by Ptolemy's youth and vulnerability. So if Arsinoe were to be replaced by Ptolemy, and Ptolemy had already made his peace with Caesar, perhaps the whole war could be wrapped up without further bloodshed. Consequently, a delegation came to Caesar saying:

> We are sick and tired of the girl [Arsinoe] and of her usurpation of the throne. Likewise we have had enough of the totally remorseless tyranny of Ganymedes. We are ready to submit to the orders of the king [Ptolemy], and if he orders us to become loyal friends of Caesar then we will do as he says and no threats could compel the people [of Alexandria] to do otherwise.

These, according to the *Alexandrine War* (ch 23) are the key words of the speech which the delegation delivered to Caesar.

The question was not whether or not Caesar believed the delegates to be sincere, because from his point of view it really did not matter. The point of keeping Ptolemy in the palace had been firstly to have a royal hostage, secondly to prevent Ptolemy from taking command of the Egyptian army and thirdly to have Egypt's potential ruler under his control.

Yet as a hostage Ptolemy had little value. In fact Arsinoe would be delighted if Caesar were to execute him and save her the trouble of doing so herself. As far as Ptolemy taking command of the Egyptian army, this was probably a good idea from the Roman perspective. Ganymedes and Arsinoe were doing an unexpectedly good job of managing the Egyptian forces and keeping the unruly Alexandrians in line (that 'remorseless tyranny' to which the delegation had referred).

If Ptolemy were to be released, even if he proved hostile, the very first thing that would happen would be a major struggle for control between him and Arsinoe, and the Egyptian army would be paralysed by the ongoing factional struggle. Afterwards, if Arsinoe came out on top, Caesar would have gained some time and otherwise be no worse off, and if Ptolemy won then Caesar would have gained some time and the Egyptians would have a measurably worse commander.

Finally, Caesar did not have to worry about releasing control of Egypt's potential ruler because he had a spare in Cleopatra – and Cleopatra was undoubtedly loyal because her fate was inextricably tied to Caesar's at this point. Releasing Ptolemy would force the young man to reveal his true colours. Should the young king prove to be an enemy of Caesar, all well and good because this would considerably simplify the question of the Egyptian succession.

Both Ptolemy and Arsinoe would have shown themselves to be enemies of Rome (well, of Caesar, but from the point of view of the Caesarians at this point Caesar and Rome were the same thing). Once Rome had regained control of Egypt this would allow Caesar, if he so wished, to instal Cleopatra on the throne alone and without any co-ruler of dubious loyalty.

Or maybe Ptolemy really had been won over by Caesar's charming personality and wanted to take command of the Egyptian forces with the sole intention of bringing the war to a close. This would be the ideal outcome, but it seemed that however things turned out, releasing Ptolemy into the wild could only be to Caesar's advantage. Caesar himself in the *Alexandrine War* claimed to be above such petty considerations, saying that he considered 'it was more noble to be conducting a war against a king than against a motley rabble.' Even the writer is dubious of such a claim remarking that Caesar's public claim was propaganda designed to make it seem 'As if it were simple nobility of spirit that led him to make this decision, instead of very careful consideration of future strategy.' (*Alexandrine War* 21)

Accordingly young Ptolemy was summoned and informed that he was going to be put back in charge of the Egyptian side, and to give some serious thought to what was best for his war-torn capital. This, Ptolemy was informed, was his chance to demonstrate his loyalty to Caesar and Rome by restoring a measure of sanity to his unruly subjects.

The proposal that he be sent from the Palace quarter to take command of the rest of the country moved Ptolemy to tears. These were not tears of relief that his dangerous confinement was over, Ptolemy assured Caesar, but tears of despair that he was forced to leave his friend and protector. 'As a practised deceiver who did not want to lower his nation's reputation for such conduct', the young man pretended the opposite of what he felt, and tearfully begged that he might stay, claiming that 'just the sight of Caesar was dearer to him than his kingdom'. (Ibid.)

Our sources do not explain how either party got through this little farce without gagging on the evident humbug, but Caesar assured the king that if he really felt that way than they would be seeing one another again very soon. Then he probably went off to check that his defences were secure against the assault that would probably be forthcoming within hours. This is indeed what happened – once released Ptolemy immediately began waging war against Caesar with an energy that suggests the release of strong feelings pent-up during his confinement.

At this point we have no word of what became of Arsinoe or Ganymedes. In fact we never hear of Ganymedes again, and given his unpopularity with both the Romans and the Alexandrians we can assume that his survival time was measured by the speed with which he abandoned his command and fled once he heard of Ptolemy's release. Arsinoe survived the change in management, either because the Alexandrians felt the need to keep a back-up monarch handy, or because she immediately withdrew from the combat and took refuge in Asia Minor where she appeared to have some support (according to Appian's *Civil Wars* 5.1.9). It may also be that Arsinoe still commanded the loyalty of a faction strong enough that Ptolemy was compelled to tolerate her presence, since he could not afford to fight a civil war against her alongside the war he was waging against Caesar.

If there ever was a genuine peace party on the Alexandrian side, its members melted away beneath the warlike zeal of the new commander. Nevertheless, Ptolemy's assumption of command was far from the occasion of universal rejoicing on the Egyptian side. Caesar was not the only one who had noticed that Ptolemy's enthusiasm for shedding Roman blood was far greater than his ability to bring this about.

The army quickly decided that it preferred the brutal competence of Ganymedes to the constantly changing orders of a young commander who had no idea what he was doing. Caesar's men seemed totally undismayed by Ptolemy's sudden change from Caesar's greatest fan to his worst enemy – in fact the Alexandrians were chagrined to discover that the legionaries found the whole business greatly amusing. Overall then, the change in command left the Romans no weaker, and the Alexandrians no stronger. Far from dismaying the Romans, it was the Egyptians who became somewhat more demoralized by Ptolemy's escape from Roman custody and restoration to his rightful place at the head of Egypt's army.

On both sides attention now turned to the reinforcements approaching Alexandria. It seems that throughout this later phase of the war some reinforcements had been arriving in Egypt in dribs and drabs as commanders of local garrisons elsewhere received the news that Caesar was in dire need of troops. One problem which faced these reinforcements was their lack of knowledge of the locality around Alexandria. These ships were eventually guided to their destination by signal fires. Only when the men landed did they discover that they had been victims of a cunning Egyptian ruse and had been led straight into the arms of the enemy, who promptly took them prisoner.

Small-scale reinforcements could be dealt with in this manner, but it was only a matter of time before a more substantial force arrived. This force was led by one Mithridates of Pergamon. Pergamon was a city-state on the west coast of Asia Minor which had been a Roman province for almost a century. However, in the chaos of the civil war, control seems to have slipped into the hands of an energetic and charismatic individual, who was widely believed to be the son of a more famous Mithridates – Mithridates VI of Pontus, often called 'Mithridates the Great' to distinguish him from the dozen or more Mithridati who were about in this era.

Mithridates of Pergamon did nothing to dispute this claimed parentage, and actually had coins struck emphasising his relationship, and he further alleged that he had inherited the armour of Mithridates the Great. His title of 'king' was more dubious because one does not become king of a Roman province, but Mithridates got around this by claiming the kingship of the neighbouring state of Galatia, which was at this time still nominally independent. However, the main claim of legitimacy for 'King' Mithridates was that he was a committed Caesarian, which was rare in a region which had mostly supported the Republican cause.

When Caesar had made his lightning tour through Anatolia in pursuit of Pompey, Mithridates had been charged with raising auxiliary forces in Syria and Cilicia to help in bringing the region back under control. Mithridates had set about the job with his customary energy and alacrity, and consequently had most of a small army together when he received urgent messages from Caesar informing him that he and his new recruits were urgently needed in Alexandria.

At this point Mithridates had no idea who commanded the seas around Alexandria, and so opted for a safer but slower approach by land. He did however dispatch several galleys loaded with supplies to give Caesar some immediate relief. It was the pending arrival of these galleys which now occupied the thoughts of both Caesar and Ptolemy.

The Egyptians were nursing the hope that news of the arrival of the galleys had not yet reached Caesar, although one wonders how a people practised in the arts of palace intrigue might have imagined that was going to happen. Cleopatra had certainly established a network of spies within the opposition camp, not just after her arrival in Alexandria, but in the years before that also. In fact, the conduct of both sides through the entire war makes it clear that anything known to the Egyptians was soon afterwards known to the Romans and vice versa.

As it might be, the situation was that the Egyptians, hoping to intercept Caesar's resupply convoy before the Romans knew that it was coming, set up a naval ambush at the town of Canopus. This town lay on the eastern part of the Nile Delta some 20km from Alexandria itself. The crews set to stage the ambush were probably delighted by the news, for Canopus had earned itself a reputation as a hard-partying town infamous for its decadence. (In later centuries, the Emperor Hadrian was so taken by the place that when he built himself a luxury retreat outside Rome at Tivoli, one section was designed as a mini-Canopus.)

In due course Caesar was informed of both the impending arrival of supplies and of the Egyptian ships waiting to intercept them. He immediately brought his flotilla to battle stations, but (possibly with his recent dip in Eunostos Harbour in mind) he decided to remain in Alexandria on this occasion. Instead, command of the fleet was given to one Tiberius Nero, whose presence with Caesar in Alexandria has not heretofore been mentioned.

Tiberius Nero, as the name indicates, was an aristocrat of the highest standing. His family were the gens Claudia which had produced leading Romans almost from the start of the Republican era and which was to become one half of the Julio-Claudian dynasty in the early Imperial era. In fact, this Tiberius Nero would go on in six years' time to father Rome's second emperor, Tiberius Claudius Caesar Augustus (adopted). Tiberius Nero was serving as Caesar's quaestor, a position in which a young man – usually an aristocrat – served a senior general as a sort of glorified paymaster while observing and learning how the business of running an army was handled.

Often when someone such as Tiberius Nero was put in a senior role such as this, there was a veteran who was quietly sent with him to 'guide' his decisions. In this case the obvious suspect would be Euphranor, the commander of the Rhodian contingent of warships which had so distinguished itself in the battle in Eunostos Harbour 'without whom no naval action was fought, and none that did not end in a decisive victory'. (*Alexandrine War* 25)

Given the ease of two-way communication between the warring parties in Alexandria, it came as no surprise to the Romans that, just as they had known of the Egyptian ambush, the Egyptians had known that the Roman flotilla was on its way and had drawn up their fleet to receive them. It is probably at this point in the war that we should add the detail (supplied in Dio 42.40) that Tiberius Nero (and Euphranor) took the opportunity of the fleet being out of the harbour to run a quick errand up the Nile. The purpose of the detour was to locate and destroy the base where Roman ships carrying reinforcements had been lured into Egyptian hands by fake signal fires.

We are informed that the Egyptians had originally planned to use only light-armed vessels in the convoy interception, yet the first warship mentioned in the resultant battle was a quadrireme, which is about as heavy as a regular ancient warship could get. Evidently the attack on their base on the Nile had given the Egyptians some indication of the Roman strength and this had resulted in some hasty reinforcements being thrown into the battle zone.

Undeterred, Euphranor immediately launched himself into the conflict and rammed an enemy ship. Having put this opponent out of action, he immediately selected his next victim and charged after that. The problem with this gallant charge was that it took up all of Euphranor's attention, which left Tiberius Nero in charge of a fleet he was not really equipped to handle. An experienced commander would have immediately observed Euphranor's intention and ordered other ships to follow into the gap created by Euphranor's charge and so broken the enemy line.

By the time that this occurred to Tiberius Nero it was too late and Euphranor's ship had vanished into the midst of the enemy fleet, where it was promptly surrounded. There the embattled Euphranor went down along with his ship, probably cursing the inexperienced

Tiberius Nero with his last breath. Thereafter it seems that both sides broke off from the action, and though history reports nothing further of this skirmish, this reticence is itself significant – Caesar never lingers too long on discussions of his setbacks. In short it seems that the Romans were beaten back and the supply convoy retreated from the fight and rejoined the army of the advancing Mithridates of Pergamon.

Certainly the Romans did not suffer a severe defeat, because we hear (from Suetonius in his biography of the Emperor Tiberius) that Tiberius Nero remained in command of the flotilla and was later rewarded for his services with a priesthood – something which would not have happened if he had allowed a significant number of Caesar's desperately-needed ships to be sent to the sea bottom.

The supply column would have now rejoined Mithridates who was squaring up to meet that first obstacle which confronted any army approaching Egypt by land. This was the fortress city of Pelusium which in previous centuries had to hold off Assyrians, Persians and the Seleucid empire. Not for nothing was Pelusium called 'the key to the defence of Egypt'.

It will be recalled that Cleopatra and her army were attempting to batter their way into Egypt at Pelusium when her private war with Ptolemy was rudely interrupted by the arrival of Pompey. Pompey was killed and Caesar had ordered Cleopatra to disband her army and join him in Alexandria. Thereafter Achillas had taken care to strengthen the garrison at Pelusium before he himself returned to Alexandria to become victim of Arsinoe's coup.

Logically, given the strength of the place, the obvious way to take Pelusium was through siege, since the changing coastline had long since isolated the city from the sea and it could be relatively easily approached on all sides. Once surrounded, the garrison was trapped within the city walls and could be induced to surrender by blood-curdling threats. This is exactly what Alexander the Great had done when he brought Egypt under Macedonian control and what

Cleopatra was attempting to do when she was interrupted, first by Ptolemy and his army, then by Pompey and Caesar.

However, Mithridates was no Alexander, and the garrison might have been hoping that, given his urgent need to get to the beleaguered Romans in Alexandria, Mithridates would be prepared to bypass them altogether. That was not going to happen because Mithridates was not foolish enough to leave a large enemy force sitting across his line of supply. With the garrison obstinately refusing to surrender, Mithridates took the only option available to him under the circumstances. He ordered his army to storm the place, reckoning that a timely arrival in Alexandria with a somewhat dilapidated army was better than arriving too late with the army intact.

Accordingly Mithridates prepared his attack in a manner which would have impressed a more experienced commander. His rationale was that even the most stubborn defender can only keep fighting for so long without a reprieve, while his own army, thanks to its overwhelming strength in numbers, could keep fighting for much longer. Therefore, he planned to assault the city from all sides with as many men as he could get to the walls at one time.

The first problem was that, while Pelusium was partly accessible by land, to surround the place for an attack on all sides, Mithridates would have to transport some of his men to the far side of the city – or to put it another way, he needed to move part of his army on to the other side of the Peleusian bottleneck before he could remove the cork. The obvious way to do this was to sail around the city and land troops on the other side. However, by the first century BC Pelusium was already partly landlocked, and access to the city was by way of the river and a canal which had been dug through the expanding shore. The Egyptians were well aware of their attacker's intentions and had blocked the river entrance with a wall of ships.

This led Mithridates to exploit one of the characteristics of ancient shipping – not only merchant ships but also quite substantial warships could be transported overland if necessary. In fact, for centuries ships had been avoiding rounding the Peloponnese in Greece by effecting a land crossing by way of Corinth. Therefore, it was only a matter of logistics – though somewhat complex logistics arranged at speed – for Mithridates to get his ships on to log runners and drag them overland. To make the operation all the more impressive it was accomplished by night. The whole operation was apparently accomplished without the Egyptians discovering what Mithridates was up to until the next day when the ships of the river blockade were attacked simultaneously from the river side and the canal. Once the blockade had been broken up Mithridates was able to accomplish his original purpose and attack Pelusium from all sides simultaneously.

The defenders of Pelusium fought off the first attack only to find that Mithridates rotated these attackers out of the battle and immediately sent in a fresh wave, and as that assault faltered due to wounds and exhaustion, a third wave immediately went in to be replaced in time by the original set of attackers who had by now gained their second wind.

This stubborn and unrelenting attack went on for a day, and by the end of it the garrison of Pelusium had been beaten into submission. According to the historian Josephus, the first breach in the walls was created by the leader of the contingent of Jewish troops whom Mithridates had collected on his sweep through the Levant. This was a man called Antipater 'who first pulled down a part of the wall and so opened a way so that the rest of the army might get access to the city'. (Josephus *Ant.* 14.8.1) The survivors were rounded up and the fortress was re-garrisoned with men loyal to Mithridates. From there the march of the relief column towards Alexandria had more in common with a victory parade than an invasion.

The main reason for this was that while the Alexandrians cared passionately about who ruled them, the Egyptian people as a whole were a great deal more indifferent. Theirs was an ancient land that had seen dynasties come and go by the dozen. For generations now Egypt had been ruled by foreigners, be they Nubian, Persian or Macedonian, and the Egyptians did not greatly care for any of them. It also helped Mithridates that there was a substantial Jewish population in many Egyptian cities, and the presence of a Jewish contingent in his army helped to bring the Jewish and from there the rest of the locals around to, if not friendship, at least tolerance of the invading force. The rural Egyptians really didn't care enough to react otherwise.

Even Ptolemy I, who at least had the decency to pretend to be more Egyptian than the Egyptians, had gained only grudging acceptance. In the ancient capitals of Thebes and Memphis the Egyptians still remembered the days of Egypt's glory under great leaders such as Ramesses II, and these memories had inspired several serious nationalist uprisings. Generally speaking, the Ptolemies had managed to keep the Egyptians under control by giving up much of their control to Egypt's ancient priestly caste, but the result was to separate the governed even further from their rulers.

For the average Egyptian it mattered not at all whether Ptolemy or Cleopatra was on the throne or both or neither. Far from seeing Mithridates as the leader of an enemy force on the sacred soil of the motherland, the weary Egyptians regarded him and his army as yet another player in a game of thrones that had very little to do with them or their everyday lives. Consequently, as the author of the *Alexandrine War* puts it:

> He [Mithridates] marched to join forces with Caesar in Alexandria. On the way he peacefully subdued those areas he passed through and brought them over to allegiance to Caesar by that authority which belongs to the winning side.
>
> (*Alexandrine War* 26)

It did not take Ptolemy long to discover that Mithridates had broken through at Pelusium. His first response was to send out a reconnaissance in force which was led by one Dioscorides. It is probable that his orders were not to take on the enemy in a direct battle but only to take the measure of the approaching force. The result from the dispatch of this force was certainly informative, but not in a way that would have brought much comfort to Ptolemy or his advisors. Mithridates learned that Dioscorides was on his way – probably with the help of friendly natives – and prepared an ambush. The Egyptians walked right into it and were destroyed.

News of this setback resulted not in a re-alignment of priorities in the Ptolemaic camp, but in an added urgency to those priorities already in place. The basic objective remained the same – to winkle Caesar out of his holdout on the Lachias Peninsula. Since Caesar's stubborn legionaries prevented the Alexandrians from forcibly doing this, the alternative was to keep Caesar cut off from reinforcements and supplies until his army was worn down by hunger and attrition.

The Alexandrians had built a fleet in record time for precisely this purpose – to interdict any supplies sent to Caesar by sea. The death of Euphranor and the failure of the latest attempt to get supplies to Caesar showed that this approach had merit. The problem was that further reinforcements were about to reach Caesar by land, so Ptolemy's army now had a dual task – they had to keep Caesar contained while simultaneously fighting off a relief attempt. Caesar on the Lachias Peninsula might have felt grim recognition of the situation that was developing.

In 52 BC Caesar had been in the same situation as Ptolemy was now. He had bottled up the Gallic leader Vercingetorix in the fortress town of Alesia, and having failed to winkle Vercingetorix out by force he had settled down to try to take Alesia by siege, reckoning that hunger and attrition might succeed where his legionaries had failed. Vercingetorix had sent urgent messages requesting reinforcements and the Gauls had gathered together a substantial army that marched to the aid of their besieged commander. In this case the Gauls had failed and hunger had forced Vercingetorix to surrender. However, given his supreme self-confidence it is doubtful that Caesar felt that history would repeat itself now that he was in the same position as Vercingetorix.

Nevertheless, just as the advance of the Gallic army to break the siege at Alesia marked the climax to Caesar's Gallic war, it was clear that the advance of Mithridates on Alexandria had brought the struggle in Alexandria to a new and crucial phase.

Chapter 10

War Alongside the Nile

Even as Mithridates and his relief force moved towards Alexandria, Ptolemy must still have felt a degree of confidence. In Gaul, Caesar had been forced to build a double set of walls – one to keep Vercingetorix in and the other to keep the relief force out – but in Egypt nature had done Ptolemy's work for him. Approaching Alexandria from the east, Mithridates had necessarily to cross the Nile, and then cross it again and again, for the river split into multiple channels as it approached the sea. It was at one of these points on the delta – confusingly at a point called Delta – that Ptolemy decided to make a stand. At that point a major branch of the Nile split into two, and Mithridates seemed to be preparing to cross just before the river did so.

The exact location of Delta has puzzled historians. Some have concluded that this spot must be where the Nile first splits into the multiple channels of the Nile Delta as a whole. This would place the site some 20 km north of where Cairo is today and around 200km from Alexandria. The argument is that Mithridates had turned his line of march southwest precisely to avoid having to fight the Egyptian forces at every river crossing along the delta, though at the cost of having made a massive detour. However, as Alexandria does not lie on one extreme of the delta, this does not explain why Mithridates would not have had the same problem crossing rivers but going south to north instead of east to west.

Another problem with a southern location is that while the writer of the *Alexandrine War* gives very few details about the site, he does specify it is not that far from Alexandria ('*non ita longe ab Alexandrea*';

Alexandrine War 27) and 200km is a fair distance even by modern standards, let alone those of the ancient world. Therefore, it seems more likely that we are looking at a sub-branch of the Nile – at *a* delta, rather than *the* delta. In fact, this is stated explicitly. '*Nomen ... pars quaedam flumen Nili derivate*' (*ibid.*) 'The name is derived from *part* of the River Nile' which splits at this point, rather than 'where the river first splits,' which would be the more logical way to put it.

The Jewish Josephus is marginally more helpful, for his heroic Antipater was still with Mithridates at this point and Josephus is keen to emphasise the role this leader of his people played in the conflict. Indeed, he bases the location of Delta on ethnic lines, saying it is not far from that location known as 'The camp of the Jews', which would give posterity a reasonably precise location if only anyone today had any idea where this camp might be. Unless archaeology unearths material from the fight, at present the best that can be offered as a location for Delta is that it is a branch of the River Nile not far from Alexandria. A further point of reference is that the river north from Delta was navigable along both of its channels as demonstrated by subsequent events.

Ptolemy had the advantage of a fleet and he used this to bring troops upriver at speed. Consequently, Mithridates arrived at Delta to find a large Egyptian force already present and prepared to fight on his side of the river, confident that the fleet could evacuate them to the westward riverbank if the action went against them. It seems that the men sent on this task were picked troops, for they were not only prepared to fight but were eager to do so. So eager in fact that they engaged with Mithridates on sight rather than wait for the arrival of the reinforcements which Ptolemy had sent upriver to join them.

At this point there is a divergence in the accounts of our two main historians Dio and the author of the *Alexandrine War*. According to Dio these Egyptian troops not only took on Mithridates but handed him a severe defeat by 'surrounding him near the lake between the river and the marsh and routing his forces.' (Dio, 42.42). The author of the *Alexandrine War* disagrees, claiming that in this instance once again Mithridates acted with a discretion suited to a more experienced commander. By this account Mithridates did not fight at all. Rather than rush into a battle before he knew the size and nature of the enemy force, he instead backed off and took up a defensive position in his camp. (Evidently he had learned from Caesar in Asia Minor that the Romans built a fortified camp at the end of every day's march and he had done the same.)

One way of squaring these two accounts is to recognize that although the *Alexandrine War* is generally the more comprehensive and contemporary text, the writer was an unashamed partisan of Caesar. Therefore, he might have elided a setback to the advance of Mithridates by skipping over an unfavourable action – for example if a portion of Mithridates' army was cut off, surrounded and routed as Dio later described – and skipped directly to the result, which was that Mithridates retreated to his camp with his wounded army, there to await developments.

What Mithridates doubtless considered prudence, the Egyptians interpreted as fear. They followed up recklessly on the camp, reckoning that they could secure the victory without needing to share the honour with the reinforcements on their way upriver. The brief retreat to his fortifications gave Mithridates time to have a good look at the enemy and their disposition, and he rather liked what he saw. Accordingly he let the Egyptians come right up to his walls. Then, before his opponents could get organized after their rapid advance, he sallied out and hit them with everything he had.

The abrupt change of Mithridates' army from prey to murderous predator threw the Egyptians into disorder and from there immediately into panic. They scattered, but not before taking substantial casualties. That the victory was not as crushing as it might have been was due to several factors. Firstly, the Egyptians were fighting on their home ground, and they knew where they could retreat to defensible positions and routes by which they could throw off pursuit.

This first reason was all the more relevant because Mithridates did not know the lie of the land and certainly did not want his army dispersed against a scattered enemy when he had no idea what further problems might already be making their way upriver towards him. Secondly, those Egyptians he could pursue – those who had retreated directly towards the Nile – did as expected and boarded their transports to safety across the river. Nevertheless, in this most recent contact with the forces besieging Caesar in Alexandria, Mithridates must have felt that things had gone satisfactorily.

Mithridates still had his work cut out. The enemy force opposing him probably contained a large element of Ptolemy's ex-legionaries, and these were not men to collapse at the first setback. Instead, the Egyptian force rallied and the survivors of that first bruising contact joined forces with Ptolemy's reinforcements as they arrived up the Nile. At this point both the Egyptians and Mithridates sent messengers to their respective leaders in Alexandria with dispatches bringing them up to date with events so far.

Once informed of developments, both Caesar and Ptolemy came to the same conclusion – they had to get out of Alexandria and take personal charge of the coming confrontation. For Ptolemy, leaving Alexandria was a relatively straightforward business. He had only to follow the route taken by the rest of his force and sail up the Nile. The only question he had to consider was how to deploy the substantial fleet he had under his command. The first option was to proceed upstream with only a few ships and use the remainder to keep Caesar penned in the Lachias Peninsula. The second option was to take everything with him, and this was the option which Ptolemy chose.

Militarily this was probably the right choice. For a start, without Ptolemy present and with a highly-motivated Roman force attempting a breakout under the personal direction of Caesar himself, there was a fair chance that Ptolemy's ships might not be able to stop Caesar's flotilla anyway. In that case Caesar would be able to defeat the Egyptian army piece by piece – first destroying the fleet in

Alexandria and then moving on to the army upriver. Secondly, at this point the Egyptian priority had to be the destruction of Mithridates and his relief force.

If Mithridates could be defeated and his army scattered then Caesar's situation would be no different from when lack of manpower had originally forced him to retreat to the palace district, and he would have to retreat back there again. However, Caesar in the palace district had proven too well entrenched for his position to be taken by storm. Therefore, if the Romans and their allies were to be defeated separately, it was better to deal first with the more exposed segment – the reinforcements of Mithridates. Once Mithridates had been dealt with the process of starving Caesar out of the Lachias Peninsula could resume.

In dealing with Mithridates the fleet could be useful in several ways, assuming the Egyptians could keep the battle close to the Nile. Firstly, several shiploads of men could be kept just offshore as a strategic reserve – completely safe from attack yet able to be landed at the right place at the right time to influence the battle. Secondly a ship just offshore made a splendid missile platform from which banks of archers could shoot arrows right over the heads of their own men into the enemy. Finally – as already demonstrated, the ships allowed a safe retreat for any troops under extreme pressure. Overall, then, it made sense for Ptolemy to take his ships with him to the coming battle and leave Caesar to follow as best as he could.

Caesar also wanted to bring his ships, but he wanted his flotilla to avoid a pitched battle on the river itself, as was logical enough since his military strength lay with the legions and these fought best on dry land. Fortunately, it was none too hard for him to do this. As mentioned earlier, Mithridates had arrived at a point which was called Delta because this was where one section of the Nile split into two major branches. Ptolemy and his fleet were making their way up one branch of the river, so Caesar had to sail out of Alexandria and along the coast until he came to one of the mouths where the second branch reached the sea.

By now the Roman fleet was a compact, battle-hardened unit, so Caesar made good time on his trip upriver. Haste was necessary because Caesar knew he was not going to be able to beat Ptolemy to the site of the coming confrontation at Delta. Nevertheless, he needed to get to Mithridates with his army before Ptolemy could attack with his now greatly superior force. In the end it was a close-run boat race. The Egyptians had a good start because theirs was the shorter route, but they had the larger fleet and army. Furthermore, Caesar had by now had considerable practice at loading his men on and off his flotilla in a hurry while the Egyptian operation was not as slick.

So Ptolemy managed to reach Delta before Caesar, but he had barely arrived and started to set up his camp when the Romans arrived – doubtless to the considerable relief of Mithridates, who was by that time severely outnumbered. Caesar promptly disembarked his men and proceeded to advance to contact with the enemy overland. Caesar's reasoning is straightforward here, as proceeding any further with his flotilla risked a naval action. The outcome of such a battle was uncertain given Ptolemy's stronger fleet and Caesar was confident that his legions were capable of beating any force in the known world so long as they had dry ground beneath their feet.

Caesar's approach to the coming engagement was that which any Roman general of the past 200 years would have recognized, for it made up in effectiveness anything it lacked in subtlety. Basically, a Roman commander looking for a quick victory would point his army at something the enemy would feel compelled to defend and march straight for it. At some point the enemy army would interpose itself between the Romans and their objective, and the Romans would steamroller through the defending army, capturing their objective and demolishing the enemy army at the same time. Surrender terms could then be agreed.

(One reason why Rome could not conquer Germany in the imperial army was that the diversified nature of German society gave the Romans no clear objective to march toward, and certainly there were none that the Germans would risk defeat to defend. Therefore the Germans fought when and if they pleased, and could retreat without the Romans gaining anything more important than healthy exercise from marching further into the forests.)

In Caesar's case there was a clear objective – Ptolemy's camp, and so he proceeded directly toward that. Ptolemy had foreseen this and taken the appropriate countermeasures. Basically, he planned to use the same tactics that were planned against the march of Mithridates, which was to contest the river crossings. Or river crossing in this case, because there was only one, some 7 miles from the Egyptian camp. Fortunately, this location was a good one from a defender's point of view.

Because this river crossing was militarily relevant, the *Alexandrine War* gives some more clues which might one day reveal Delta's location. For a start the tributary was narrow but it ran through very steep banks, which suggests that it had held that course for some time (and may do so still). Secondly there were a number of good-sized trees in the vicinity, which is certainly not the case all along the Nile. This long, deep branch of the Nile served as a defensive ditch over which Caesar would have to force a contested crossing. Ptolemy's problem was that while there were no good crossing points, Caesar had a multitude of bad crossing points to choose from and the Egyptians did not know which he would attempt.

Therefore Ptolemy hesitated to send out his heavy infantry, presumably worried that if Caesar forced a crossing up or downstream from his army then there was a danger that the legions might do an end run around the Egyptian heavy infantry and strike directly at the camp. Instead Ptolemy reckoned that the natural trench was strong enough a defence that it could be held by missile troops alone, and he accordingly sent out light infantry capable of moving at speed to whichever crossing point Caesar attempted. He also sent all of his cavalry so that this even more mobile force could hold back any Roman attempts to bridge the ditch before the infantry arrived.

Caesar took a dim view of this. 'An unfair engagement, since the position allowed no rewards for bravery or any consequences for cowardice.' (*Alexandrine War* 29). Just as importantly, Caesar's men shared this opinion. They had been penned in Alexandria for weeks, fighting street battles against irregular (but highly motivated) infantry, and had been forced to fight semi-aquatic engagements on unfamiliar ground where their tactical skills were less valuable. The legionaries were somewhat tired of all this and were looking for a chance to engage their enemies on level ground and give a demonstration of what they did best. The situation on the riverbank was more like that in Alexandria – rather than the direct confrontation the Romans craved, they were again on difficult ground with enemies hurling missiles at them from unreachable positions.

Caesar's cavalry immediately scattered out along the bank looking for opportunities to ford the river. These cavalry were not Roman but German and, like the Sixth Legion, they had been with Caesar since before the civil war. Their exact tribe is uncertain, though there was probably a core of riders from the Tencteri, a people known for their warlike ways and superb horsemanship.

Caesar had obtained the first of his German cavalrymen in an unusual manner. In 58 and 55 BC he had beaten back German attacks upon his new conquest of Gaul. Once he had defeated the German invaders, he demanded hostages from them to ensure future good behaviour. These hostages were high-ranking tribesmen who therefore came complete with their own sets of bodyguards and retainers. Overall there were some 400 of these men, and many of the retainers were mercenaries who were there for money rather than from personal loyalty. (Other German mercenaries served Herod of Judea and, in later years, Caligula of Rome.) These men were happy to fight for Caesar while their former masters were incarcerated.

It soon became clear that the German horsemen were superior to their Gallic counterparts, and also to the Spanish troops who also made up a large part of Caesar's cavalry. Caesar responded by replacing the Germans' ponies with larger and stronger steeds and using the men as his main strike force in cavalry actions. In the war with the Gallic leader Vercingetorix, these German cavalry were key in preventing Gallic attacks on Caesar's supply trains.

Like the Sixth Legion, the German cavalry accompanied Caesar across the Rubicon and into Rome's civil war. In several actions, such as outside Dyrrhachium in 48 BC, the Germans fought on foot and proved that their main asset was not their horsemanship but their pure ferocity. In Alexandria there was little call for the Germans as cavalry, and though they must have fought alongside Caesar's legionaries in the street battles in that siege, there was no reason to take special note of their performance.

However, once out in relatively open country the German mercenaries once more came into their own. Caesar had brought their horses with them, and once they hit Egyptian resistance on the riverbank the Germans quickly fanned out up and downstream to look for breaks in the steep banks which might allow access to the river, which they were quite capable of crossing once given the opportunity. In fact, on this occasion the Germans and their horses are recorded as swimming across where they found places too deep to ford. Because the cavalry operated as small pockets of men they were able to infiltrate across the river in groups, unopposed by the Egyptian commander who presumably wanted to keep his (curiously ineffective) cavalry together as a single unit.

Caesar's legionaries meanwhile had worked out their own way of getting across the river. As mentioned earlier, there were several stands of tall trees nearby. If this was a rare occurrence along the Nile it now became somewhat rarer as the Romans cut the trees down and threw the trunks across the narrowest parts of the river. They then closed ranks and charged across these impromptu bridges into the Egyptian ranks.

Ptolemy had predicated his defence on the fact that Caesar's heavy infantry would be held on the far bank of the river and so he had sent only light infantry and cavalry to hold the line. The cavalry were by now presumably deployed to keep the German horsemen off the flanks of the Egyptian missile troops who therefore had to try to hold off the infantry attack on their own.

It proved an unequal struggle – the Egyptian troops were lightly armoured and carried bulky bows and javelins unsuited to close combat. Caesar's legions were heavily armoured, highly motivated and very good at their job. Once they had a bridgehead over the river, the battle was effectively over and the only option available to the Egyptian light infantry was to flee back to their camp.

This, under normal circumstances, would have been possible with the cavalry covering their retreat, but once again the Egyptian cavalry are conspicuously absent. Either they had engaged the German mercenaries and been routed, or the Egyptian cavalry commander decided that cowardice was the better part of valour and led the retreat, leaving the light infantry to their fate. This fate was gruesome as the legionaries had a considerable degree of frustration to get out of their systems. 'Few survived to take refuge with their king [at his camp]. Almost all of the others were cut down.' (*Alexandrine War* 29)

If one is going to fight against a man generally acknowledged as one of the best generals in the known world, it behoves that man's opponent to make sure that he has a very well-defended base. This is especially true if that great general also has very experienced soldiers under his command who quite certainly count themselves – with good reason – as also being the best in the world. In acknowledgement of these facts, the Egyptian army was ensconced in what might be fairly described as Fort Ptolemy. Ptolemy had selected a naturally strong position on high ground between the Nile and a marsh formed by overflow from the river. Behind his camp the ground rose even higher and became too broken for troops to advance without difficulty. The camp was therefore secure on three sides with the only remaining approach being that on the fourth side parallel to the river.

Once Ptolemy had seen the fate which befell his light infantry in the field (we never hear what became of the cavalry) he made it plain that he had no intention of coming out to fight. If Caesar wanted Ptolemy and his army he would have to fight his way into the camp to get them – or in a neat reversal of fortune, Ptolemy would stand pat behind secure fortifications and hope for reinforcements just as Caesar had until recently been doing in Alexandria.

There was one problem with Ptolemy's secure location and this is summarized by an old army proverb which was probably extant even in Caesar's time – 'If you make it too hard for them to get in, then you can't get out.' Ptolemy had boxed himself in, with three escape routes blocked and a vengeful Roman army powering its way up the fourth.

All this Caesar observed as he approached the Egyptian camp. Caesar allowed his men to chase the remnants of the Egyptian light infantry right up to the ramparts because he wanted it to be clear that he had defeated them comprehensively. How the remainder of Ptolemy's army reacted to the sight of their defeated and terrified comrades sprinting for safety and to the legionaries bearing down upon them at speed would be a useful test of the Egyptian morale.

However, Caesar had no intention of letting his men go straight on to attacking Ptolemy's camp. His men were tired after their pursuit of the light infantry and the hasty journey up the Nile had probably been none too comfortable as well. The hopeful possibility that the Egyptians might panic and flee at Caesar's approach had not materialized – possibly because, however much they might feel like doing so, the Egyptians had nowhere to run.

Therefore, with the enemy manning the ramparts and to all appearances ready, willing and able to resist, Caesar signalled his men to pull back and pitch camp. After all, Caesar knew where the enemy were and his camp was close enough to ensure that they were not going anywhere. Therefore, it was best to let the Egyptians stew over their prospects for the coming confrontation. If we are to believe Dio, the Egyptians were indeed stewing. It had finally dawned on Ptolemy that he was in a precarious position – hemmed in his camp and about to take on the best general in the known world. Belatedly the young pharaoh dispatched envoys to Caesar to see if a peace deal could be worked out.

These diplomatic overtures came far too late and they fell on deaf ears. As far as Caesar was concerned, the time for negotiations had been well over a month ago. In the opinion of the exasperated Roman commander, the entire Alexandrian War had gone on for too long already. In the coming days, beside Ptolemy's camp on the banks of the Nile, things were going to be resolved once and for all – and there was no need for any discussion about how this was going to be accomplished.

Chapter 11

The Final Showdown

Overnight both sides probably took stock of the situation. The Roman and Egyptian armies were now approximately equal in numbers, if not in strength. We do not know how many of his troops Caesar left behind to garrison the Lachias Peninsula in Alexandria, but we can assume that this garrison was the bare minimum. After all Caesar still had the superb observation post of the Great Lighthouse and his men stationed there would have earlier reported to him that the majority of the Egyptian army had pulled out to deal with the approaching threat of Mithridates and his army.

Therefore Caesar was able to reduce his own defending force to an even greater degree. This was because it takes fewer men to defend a position than are needed to attack it, and even fewer when the attackers are not veteran troops but unskilled amateur Alexandrians. Furthermore, by now everyone remaining in the city was well aware that the outcome of the war was going to be decided somewhere upriver, so there was little point in wasting lives in Alexandria itself – especially as the leaders were no longer present to urge their side on.

It is safe to assume then that most of the Sixth Legion – or what remained of it – were with Caesar, and probably elements of the Twenty-seventh were left to garrison the Lachias Peninsula in Alexandria. Certainly the speed, determination and improvisation of the legionaries at the river bank is indicative of veteran troops such as the Sixth rather than the recruits of the Twenty-seventh. The German cavalry we already know Caesar had with him.

Apart from that very hard core, it is uncertain what troops Caesar had at his disposal. At a rough estimate there were some 20,000 of them under three different commanders. Apart from his own legionaries there were the men whom Mithridates had recruited immediately after Caesar's victory at Pharsalus and others whom he had swept up as he advanced southward to the relief of his embattled commander in Alexandria. The most substantial of these latter troops were the Jewish contingent under Antipater the Idumean.

It has already been seen that Antipater had played a crucial part in the capture of the fortress town of Pelusium. Antipater was strongly committed to being as helpful to Caesar as he possibly could because, before Caesar's victory at Pharsalus, Antipater had been just as helpful a supporter of Pompey, and had remained so until the latter's unfortunate demise in Egypt. Therefore, Antipater had a lot to make up for, and he intended to do this by assisting Caesar to get out of his Alexandrian predicament.

Exactly what weapons and armour Antipater's men were using is uncertain. Ever since the collapse of the Seleucid empire the Levant had been in a somewhat chaotic state, so it is probable that most of these men were experienced in warfare. It is known that Antipater's son, Herod the Great, employed Thracian and Galatian mercenaries so these might have already been present.

In the time of the Maccabees, a hundred years previously, the Jewish people had produced troops capable of taking on Seleucid regulars – indeed, they were one of the reasons that the Seleucid empire had collapsed in the first place. So, for Antipater's contingent, we can hypothesize a mixture of mercenaries using native equipment and a majority of soldiers somewhere between heavy infantry and light troops – that is, men with swords and shields, but only basic body armour.

As to the rest of the army of Mithridates these would, like Antipater's men, have been representative of the communities from which they were drawn. Greek cities in the region would have supplied peltasts – men armed with throwing spears and one long stabbing spear – and perhaps a small contingent of phalangites who could be assembled into a small, but formidable, phalanx. There would have been a reasonable contingent of light missile troops (slingers had been in the region before the time of King David, and Syrian archers were later a staple element in Rome's imperial armies).

Finally, there were those elements of the army of Cleopatra which we can imagine the queen had been attempting to re-assemble. Caesar's order that the armies of Cleopatra and Ptolemy be disbanded had proven a nearly disastrous mistake, as it had left only one army in the region – that now commanded by Ptolemy. If Cleopatra had sent orders to her army that they should forget the command to disband and return immediately to the standards, at least some would have complied. Cleopatra's supporters in the countryside would have recruited whoever else they could, though this probably did not add up to a significant contribution.

To resist Caesar's attack, Ptolemy had his own hard core of legionaries – the soldiers brought by Gabinius who had since made Egypt their home. These men were accustomed to lording it over the locals and bitterly resented that Cleopatra had sent some of them to die for Pompey's cause at Pharsalus. Having nailed their colours to the Egyptian mast these veteran soldiers were probably the best-trained and most highly motivated of Ptolemy's troops.

Many of the remaining soldiers were also professionals called *misthophoroi* – troops recruited in Egypt from the native population. These men formed units of regular soldiers, though by now the Macedonian phalanx of the early Ptolemies had proven impractical for the type of warfare in the later Ptolemaic era and had been abandoned. The ethnic composition of these units was often given as 'Greek' or 'Persian', though this ethnic designation was somewhat dubious by Cleopatra's time – as demonstrated by an abundance of contemporary hybrid Greek-Egyptian names later discovered by archaeologists.

For centuries the Ptolemies had been recruiting mercenaries from abroad and when these men were discharged from service they were settled on plots of land within Egypt to become reserve soldiers called *kleroi*. These men and their successors were liable for military call-ups and retained their original ethnic designation, though several generations of Egyptian wives meant that these men were probably very little different from their 'native' counterparts. They were armed with sword, shield, javelins and wore a light cuirass and helmets, the latter probably mass-produced by factories in Alexandria.

Usually, the army also had a substantial contingent of bowmen and light javelineers, but after recent events at the riverbank this element of the army was much reduced. The *Alexandrine War* informs us that Ptolemy had sent 'all his cavalry' to support the missile troops at the riverbank, and the last we hear of this element is when they left the Ptolemaic camp – thereafter they effectively evaporate.

Given that the farmer-soldiers of Egypt had been given a secondary role to mercenaries in recent years, it is probable that most of the native cavalry were used mainly for policing and routine patrols. The prospect of fighting Caesar's fierce German mercenaries for a king about whom very few felt much devotion might have been a strong incentive for many of these cavalrymen to take the chance to head straight for home once they were out of Ptolemy's camp.*

Evidently Ptolemy himself was unconvinced that his men were prepared to fight and die for him on the battlefield, and he was realistic enough about his own capabilities to know that he was no Caesar. His best strategy was therefore exactly the one he had chosen – to stay within the walls of his camp. With ramparts between themselves and the Romans, his men would fight more enthusiastically, and there was always the hope that after a few setbacks Caesar's hybrid army would fall apart.

Ptolemy's own army was probably going to stay together simply because it had nowhere else to go. This theory had been given its

---

* Fischer-Bovet, C., *Army and Society in Ptolemaic Egypt*, Armies of the Ancient World (Cambridge University Press, 2014).

first test when Caesar's men had come rampaging up to the walls in pursuit of the remainder of his light infantry, and this had not caused the panic and rout that Caesar had hoped and Ptolemy feared. Nevertheless, Egyptian morale could best be described as 'fragile'.

The day after his arrival outside Ptolemy's camp, Caesar recommenced operations. He was still not ready to attack the main Egyptian defences directly but he was determined to continue his tactic of first softening the morale of the defenders. Accordingly, he drew up his entire army into battle formation and launched it into an assault – not on Ptolemy's camp but at a minor fortress in a fishing village close by. This fort had been garrisoned as an outpost of the main camp and was linked to it by a series of fortifications.

Caesar decided to take the village and its fort, not because either had any particular strategic value, but because he wanted the watching Egyptians in the main camp to have a good look at what was about to happen to them in the immediate future. The same result could have been achieved with a smaller force, but without the shock and awe factor created by the sight of a Roman army in battle array lining up and then steamrolling over its target before proceeding to mop up all along the way through the chain of fortifications leading to the main camp itself.

Just as this action was meant to unnerve the Egyptian army in the main camp, this opening success was intended to give Caesar's legionaries an appetite for the coming battle. Certainly the second part of this operation fulfilled its purpose, for, once the army had squashed the defences of the little fort, Caesar's men advanced enthusiastically on the main camp. The extent to which the defenders weren't demoralized was demonstrated by the hail of javelins which stopped the advancing troops in their tracks. There followed a brisk exchange of missile fire while Caesar and his lieutenants tried to work out the best way of cracking this particular nut.

As previously noted, the Egyptian camp had natural defences on three sides. An attack across the marsh was out of the question, and the rocky ground rising above the camp was an unappealing prospect – quite apart from the fact that Caesar would have to shift his army around to get there. Therefore, the options were to stage a direct frontal attack or to attempt to insinuate a strong force between the Nile and the camp ramparts on that side. Obviously, the latter option was highly risky. Nevertheless, in the end Caesar opted for this, but in conjunction with an attack on the open side of the camp which would hopefully pin down the best of the Egyptian defenders.

Both attacks failed to make much headway. Because the most accessible front was the most vulnerable, the cream of Ptolemy's army was charged with its defence, and here the ramparts were strongest. The attack on the river side was a miserable failure. This was firstly because there was little space to deploy, which meant that Caesar's men were crammed between the river and the walls, and easy targets for missile troops. To make things worse, these missile troops were not only on the ramparts of the camp but also on Ptolemy's ships still anchored in the Nile. These ships had been loaded with a good proportion of Ptolemy's remaining light infantry and they now lined the riverbank as floating missile barges with slingers and bowmen who could pick their targets with impunity. Caught by fire from two directions this attack faltered early and the men took the greatest number of casualties suffered by any of Caesar's troops in the entire day's action.

Had Caesar been in command of a normal Roman field army, at this point he would have pulled back and commenced regular siege operations, starting with the assembly of siege weaponry. (Generally an army carried the essential parts of such weapons and assembled the rest from local materials once they reached the place where they were needed.) However, Caesar was in no mood for a prolonged siege, especially as Ptolemy's command of the river meant that his fleet could keep feeding supplies to the army long after Caesar's men had used up all the local food reserves.

Yet one of the great strengths of a Roman army lay in its adaptability, and this adaptability was particularly powerful when the army was commanded by as intelligent and opportunistic a commander as Caesar. So far things had not been going as hoped. The attack was getting bogged down and Egyptian morale was holding up. Indeed, Egyptian morale was becoming buoyed up by success to the extent that men were leaving other parts of the camp to join in the efforts against the Romans on the ramparts and the river.

This gave Caesar his opportunity. The marsh was still impractical, but with only a skeleton garrison now holding the rocky ground at the rear of the camp, an attack on this third side had become possible, assuming the attack was made by veteran troops with a top-notch commander. Fortunately, Caesar had both.

According to the *Alexandrine War* Caesar ordered '*cohortis illo circumire castra et summum locum aggredi iussit*' ('He ordered the cohorts to go around the camp and attack the high ground', *Alexandrine War* 31). The use of the word 'cohorts' refers to elements of the regular Roman legion, which suggests that Caesar had not yet ordered the men of the Sixth into the frontal attack on the ramparts, let alone fed any into the meat-grinder on the riverbank. He had probably been keeping this elite unit in reserve for just such an opportunity as now presented itself. To command the attack he had Decimus Carfulenus, 'a man of exceptional personality and experience of warfare'.

Since the location of the Egyptian camp is now unknown, also unknown is how Carfulenus and his men managed the '*circumire castra*' part of their brief – 'getting around' the enemy camp could not have been that easy. For a start, since the troops had to get around the Ptolemaic camp, it is safe to assume that Caesar was at the open side of the camp where the attack was being pressed against the main ramparts. On one side of Caesar's position was the Nile, which was presumably impassable as Ptolemy's fleet commanded the river. Therefore, to get to the rocky heights at the back of the camp, Carfulenus and the Sixth must have circled around the marsh on the other side. This had to be done in record time, for Caesar's men were being decimated on the riverbank. Yet if the Romans were to let up with their attack on that side, the Egyptians who had been drawn into the fray would return to their original positions, which had included a strong force on the heights. So the men of the Sixth had to double-time around the marsh, climb a steep, rocky slope at high speed and then throw themselves into battle – all without the enemy noticing what they were doing until the last moment.

One way that this might have been accomplished is described by Dio. His description of the Alexandrian War is highly compressed, and as we have seen, his account of the events leading up to the battle at the camp is at times completely incompatible with that given in the *Alexandrine War*. Nevertheless, he describes a ruse whereby Caesar pretended to be withdrawing some troops down one leg of the river, but instead took soldiers 'around the lake [marsh?] and fell upon the Egyptians unexpectedly.' (Cassius Dio, *Roman History* 42.42) In short, the circumnavigation of the marsh may have been an amphibious operation disguised as a partial withdrawal. This is about all we can get from the text of Dio here, since he is otherwise confused about the location of the battle and who did what while it was going on.

In the more reliable, contemporary *Alexandrine War* the whole of this far-from-inconsiderable feat is lightly passed over in the text, which simply assumes the legionaries pulled off their race successfully and picks up the story saying 'when they arrived at their destination…'.

When the Roman troops arrived at their destination they threw themselves directly at the enemy, with predictable results. While Egyptian morale had not buckled with Caesar's earlier demonstrations of force, it had certainly been undermined. Therefore, even before the sounds of chaos erupted from the heights behind them, the troops manning the ramparts were already expecting the worst. This was immediately confirmed by the sight of Roman legionaries chasing downhill the few Egyptians who had remained to guard this supposedly secure spot to their rear.

This was the moment upon which the fate of the war now turned. A great general with excellent troops could have taken this opportunity to rip away a portion of the army defending the walls, launch a counter-charge up the hill and destroy the relatively small force that had broken through the camp's defences. This would be a crushing blow because, though small, that force represented the core of the opposing army. There was indeed a great general and excellent troops present, but unfortunately for the Egyptians, both were on the other side. All the Egyptian leadership could contribute was incoherent panic, which added to the prevailing chaos.

Those not defending the walls were aware of tumult, shouting, and the clash of weapons on all sides but had no clear idea of what was happening. Groups of men rushed about the camp – some presumably headed for where they assumed that the fighting was taking place, the more prescient grabbing what they needed for immediate flight. Studies of ancient battles have shown that nothing demoralized men fighting on the front rank more surely than the knowledge that something horrible was happening to the rest of the army behind them.

Thus the Egyptian soldiers fighting on the ramparts and beside the river were seized with the worry that, while staving off the Romans in front of them, they were going to be stabbed in the back by Romans coming up behind them. Under the circumstances it is understandable that they were to a degree distracted from the task before them – a task which required full concentration as Caesar's men had become as inspired as the Egyptians were demoralized by recent events.

The result of these combined pressures was that the defence of Ptolemy's camp imploded. The fall of the rocky heights was followed by the almost simultaneous collapse of the main rampart and the river wall. Suddenly Roman troops who had been successfully held back until moments previously were swarming over the walls from all directions and falling upon the confused Egyptian soldiery like starving wolves.

It should be remembered that even without the ramparts to defend them the Egyptians were capable of putting up a fair fight. Their number was equal to that of the attacking enemy and most of their opponents were armed and equipped much as they were themselves. The Gabinians could hold off Caesar's legionaries at least for a while, so theoretically the battle was not yet lost. In practical terms however, it was game over the moment that Caesar's legionaries took the upper slopes at the rear of the camp. The Ptolemaic army totally lost the will to fight and disintegrated into a panicked mass of men, each of whom was dedicated to saving himself alone.

With Caesar's men massacring anyone in their way, it quickly occurred to the Egyptians that their only hope of safety lay with the ships on the river, and thousands of men surged in that direction. There was a substantial drop over the camp's ramparts to the ground alongside the riverbank, but those who reached that section of the walls had no choice – they were simply shoved over by the mass of humanity pressing behind them. The fall from the walls into the trench outside was fatal for the first to fall, but thereafter the rapidly accumulating pile of corpses meant that the drop got shorter and the landing softer, so a good many thereafter managed to escape to the fleet.

Caesar had recently been in a similar situation himself in Alexandria, when he had been forced to abandon ship because it had become clear that the mass of panicked humanity pushing aboard his ship was more than the craft could handle. So Caesar must have felt a grim sense of recognition when one of the larger ships on the river became overloaded with men, dangerously unbalanced and then capsized, dumping the soldiers aboard into the Nile. Egypt being a desert country, it is doubtful that many of these soldiers could swim and the few who could had little chance to do so while weighed down by their armour and surrounded by drowning non-swimmers.

What Caesar only discovered later was that among the casualties of this shipwreck was Ptolemy himself. Later interrogation of prisoners established that in the last chaotic moments Ptolemy had been rushed from the camp and aboard the doomed ship. Thereafter the pharaoh is never mentioned again in contemporary sources, and the presumption is that his was among the hundreds of corpses swept downriver, to be either consumed by crocodiles or eventually deposited into the Mediterranean. (The Nile crocodile grows up to six metres in length and has a prodigious appetite.) There is however an alternative story written several centuries later by the historian Florus, which maintains that the body of Ptolemy was later discovered buried in mud, yet recognizable because it wore the royal coat of golden mail armour (Florus 2.13.60).

It maybe assumed that, even without corpses floating downriver, the Alexandrians were quickly aware of the disastrous outcome of the battle at the camp of the late Ptolemy. This left the question of what the citizens should do next. As the army of Ptolemy had been essentially destroyed, the tables had been turned with a vengeance. If the Alexandrians wanted to keep fighting, this time it was they who would have to stand siege, and against an enemy who was much better at conducting sieges than they themselves had been.

If we are to believe the history of Florus, then among the first to react was Ganymedes, commander of the Egyptian forces before Ptolemy took over. Ganymedes' response was to leave early and at speed – though this was to no avail for he is reported as being 'cut down while fleeing.' (Florus 2.13.60).

This left Cleopatra's sister Arsinoe as the top-ranking Ptolemy on the Egyptian side. However, there is no indication that anyone turned to her for leadership. Even with an army to back her Arsinoe had not been an effective war leader, and her forceful displacement by Ptolemy had left her with some grudges to repay. The prospect of Arsinoe returning to command and getting her vengeance probably made surrender to Caesar seem a more attractive option to those leading Egyptians who had abandoned Arsinoe for Ptolemy. All the more so because Caesar had a reputation of being generous towards enemies who surrendered promptly – while being unflinchingly brutal to those who offered resistance.

Caesar himself was well aware of the importance of seizing the moment. The Alexandrians were currently leaderless, and he had no intention of giving them time to find a new commander. Therefore he left the process of cleaning up the battlefield and re-embarking his infantry aboard ship to his subordinates. He himself headed for Alexandria overland with his cavalry to accept the surrender which the Alexandrians had not yet offered. In short, by assuming the defeat and surrender of the Egyptians, Caesar was displaying the same arrogant confidence that had got him into the Alexandrian War in the first place.

On this occasion that confidence was not misplaced. When Caesar rode up to the walls of Alexandria, taking it for granted that the garrison there would surrender, the demoralized and leaderless troops did just that. Once Caesar was within the walls and word spread that the war was over, any potential resistance collapsed. The citizens abandoned their fortifications and decided to trust their survival on Caesar's 'well-earned reputation for magnanimity' (*Alexandrine War* 32).

There was a certain convention which was followed in the Mediterranean world for occasions such as this. Those who were throwing themselves on the mercy of a conqueror would dress themselves in supplicant robes (no description of what these robes were has come down to us) and grab whatever religious symbols were likely to be of significance to the man to whom they were appealing. Then, under the dubious protection of the gods thus invoked, the supplicants would throw themselves at the feet of their conqueror and offer unconditional surrender.

Safe to say Caesar was not only prepared to accept this surrender, he was counting on it.

The alternative was to leave himself and his relatively small cavalry force alone in the midst of thousands of hostile Alexandrians. Had the populace possessed the will to continue the war they could have mobbed Caesar and his men right then and there but, as Caesar had confidently expected, repeated setbacks had destroyed their will to fight.

There was, of course, also the knowledge that the rest of Caesar's army would eventually be coming downriver and would have some very pointed questions to ask if their commander was mistreated. Overall then, the best solution for everyone was for a massive outbreak of amity. Caesar took the surrendered Alexandrian leaders 'under his protection' (which is so much nicer than taking them prisoner, which was effectively the same thing) and proceeded towards his own garrison on the Lachias Peninsula. This garrison greeted Caesar with jubilant cheers which were probably tinged with more than a touch of relief.

The Alexandrian War was over. Having wrapped up a conflict which should never have started in the first place, Caesar was free to finally leave Egypt and deal with pressing business which had been piling up elsewhere.

Chapter 12

Aftermath

While Caesar left Egypt a nominally independent nation, he also left behind a very substantial garrison to ensure that Egypt actually remained firmly under Roman control. According to Caesar's biographer Suetonius, Caesar preferred Egypt as a client kingdom rather than a Roman province. This was because he feared that Egypt's wealth and natural defences would present any governor with an unassailable base should he decide to follow the example of Caesar himself and declare war upon the government in Rome.

As well as the right bestowed by victory, Caesar had the legal authority to rearrange matters in Egypt to his personal satisfaction because while he was busy elsewhere his consulship had expired. Rather than have Caesar stand for consul *in absentia* – which would have been a violation of the few Roman electoral traditions which Caesar had not violated already – Caesar's deputy in Rome opted instead to force the Senate to appoint Caesar as dictator for the coming year of 47 BC. In fact, Caesar was so taken with the powers that came with his new position that he later appointed himself Dictator for Life.

Since it suited his purposes anyway, Caesar adhered closely to the dynastic arrangements laid out in the will of Ptolemy Auletes. As her father had wished, Cleopatra was returned to the throne as co-regent with her brother. As the brother specified by Ptolemy Auletes was missing presumed dead, Caesar replaced him with the last of the Ptolemaic males, the unimaginatively named Ptolemy XIV. This co-regent was little obstacle to the sole rule of Cleopatra, being a stripling of twelve years old. (At this time Cleopatra herself was a venerable twenty-two years of age.) It is probable, but unconfirmed, that at this point Caesar transferred rule of Cyprus to Cleopatra. Restoring this historic possession of Egypt would have gone a long way towards reconciling the Egyptian people and Alexandrians with Caesar and their new rulers.

Just to make sure that these new Egyptian rulers behaved themselves, Caesar kept hold of his Ptolemaic spare – Arsinoe – who had fallen into his hands and was now a captive. When Caesar finally returned to Rome, he celebrated a series of triumphs to mark his victories at locations across the Mediterranean world. Arsinoe was displayed in the Alexandrian category of these victory parades along with other treasures of Egypt. In a triumph it was traditional that after an enemy leader was so exhibited, that leader would then be ceremonially strangled in the dungeons below the Capitoline hill while the triumphator enjoyed a ceremonial dinner above. Caesar had done this with the Gallic leader Vercingetorix but he had no such plans for Arsinoe, who was much more valuable to him alive. Therefore, after her ritual humiliation in Rome, Arsinoe was dispatched to a temple in Ephesus in Asia Minor – close enough to Egypt to be deployed in a hurry if needed, but far enough away to prevent the princess from stirring up trouble on her own account.

Once Caesar had sorted out the affairs of Egypt to his satisfaction, both Suetonius and the historian Appian inform us that he then took himself on vacation. Both mentions are somewhat laconic. Appian rather snarkily states that Caesar 'sailed up the Nile with 400 ships, seeing the country together with Cleopatra whose company he enjoyed in other ways' (Appian, *Civil Wars* 2.90). Suetonius, who does not usually spare us any juicy gossip, is equally curt: 'He often feasted with Cleopatra until daybreak and he and she would have gone on her barge of state through Egypt right to the Ethiopian border had his soldiers not refused to follow him' (Suet. *Caesar* 52).

From these two sentences some writers have conjured a luxury cruise of degenerate debauchery, to which debauchery it has to be said that the state barge certainly lent itself. This barge was one of the type called a *thalamegos*, a massive ship equipped with every luxury. (This vessel was also later used to stun Mark Antony with its splendour when he met Cleopatra in later years.) The ship was a floating pleasure palace almost 100m long, complete with luxury bedchambers, dining rooms and viewing points strategically situated along its catamaran-style hulls.

There is no doubt that Caesar would have thoroughly enjoyed such a holiday. He had just had a stressful few months in Alexandria preceded by several stressful years before that. Also, like most Romans, Caesar was fascinated by the exotic land of Egypt and certainly would have gone as far upriver as he could. The question was whether he could have gone very far – and indeed whether this fabulous trip even happened in the first place.

On the one hand, a cruise upriver in the company of a massive fleet packed with soldiery would have certainly informed people living in the Egyptian south that the north of the country was again firmly under control. There is no indication that the Egyptians of Memphis were planning a nationalist secession as they had done on occasion in the past, but a show of unified force such as Caesar and Cleopatra now displayed would certainly have nipped any such plans in the bud.

The idea that Caesar was prepared to sail all the way to Ethiopia is certainly fanciful, even if the suggestion that his soldiers refused to follow him were not an obvious riff on the story of the soldiers of Alexander the Great refusing to follow their leader south into India three centuries previously. Caesar, the newly-minted Dictator, had an empire to run, a lively foreign invasion shaping up in Asia Minor and Republican forces gathering strength in Spain and Africa. He simply could not abandon all this for a hedonistic pleasure cruise.

Nevertheless, we do have a contemporary hint that Caesar did go missing for a while. Cicero, who had abandoned the Republican cause after Pompey's defeat at Pharsalus, wrote to his friend Atticus: 'There is a dubious rumour going around that Caesar has left Alexandria.... and this all subsequent messengers have confirmed.' (*Ad Att.* 434) Since Cicero clearly had no idea where Caesar had got to, there is a possibility that this is a reference to Caesar playing truant from his responsibilities with a riparian jaunt.

However, this trip could not have taken very long, because the chronology does not support it. Even if Caesar did some of his arranging of Egyptian affairs while aboard the state barge (very possible – the man was a workaholic notoriously disinclined to pleasures of the flesh other than the carnal) the Nile trip could have taken no more than a fortnight, and more probably a week. Any longer than this and we have to rearrange the time for Caesar's return to Asia Minor and much of the chronology of the later African War. Besides there was another reason why Caesar might not have wanted to dally too long on the banks of the Nile – Cleopatra, his paramour, was pregnant.

The child was named Caesarion. His existence must have been slightly frustrating to Caesar, who lacked a legitimate Roman successor. His only legitimate child was a daughter, Julia, who had died in childbirth. However, despite Cleopatra's later attempt to get Caesar to formally recognize and adopt the child Caesar made no attempt to do so. Nevertheless, Caesarion (who was said to have inherited many of his father's looks and mannerisms) was the heir to both the Julian and Ptolemaic bloodlines, which made him a valuable – or dangerous – piece in the high-stakes politics of the late Roman Republic.

Unlike many men who hear that they are about to become fathers, Caesar really did have to get out of town quick. In fact, he would have liked to be simultaneously in Asia Minor, Rome, Spain and North Africa as in all four places crises were either brewing or had already come to the boil. Therefore, Caesar left Cleopatra with a strong garrison and headed at speed to the nearest of these crises, which was in Asia Minor.

The Twenty-seventh Legion remained in Egypt for the present, along with many of the troops raised by Mithridates. The Pergamene leader did not retain command of these troops but appears instead to have accompanied Caesar and the Sixth Legion back to Asia Minor. The trusty (and now even more depleted) Sixth accompanied Caesar back to war, this time against the Pontic king, Pharnaces.

Like Mithridates of Pergamon, Pharnaces II of Pontus was a son of Mithridates the Great – that king who had fought Rome for most of his adult life, sometimes with considerable success. When Rome fell into the convulsion of Caesar's civil war, Pharnaces took advantage of the fact that Roman troops were withdrawn from the region to fight in Greece. He conquered points north and east, and then took his army into Anatolia. By now Caesar was in Egypt with problems of his own, so he sent his subordinate Domitius Calvinus to deal with Pharnaces and then send urgently to Egypt the troops with which he had done it.

Domitius was unable to fulfil even part one of these instructions because his first encounter with Pharnaces resulted in a defeat. Things might have been even worse had Pharnaces not had to pull back to deal with a rebellion in his homeland. This allowed Domitius to belatedly send the Twenty-seventh to Caesar's aid (p.82) but the loss of this legion left him stretched thin in Asia Minor. As a result when Pharnaces returned to the offensive, Domitius was forced to retreat.

Once he had concluded his business in Alexandria, Caesar headed for Asia Minor at high speed. His arrival and the arrival of his veteran legionaries was very bad news for Pharnaces. The Pontic king attempted to open negotiations, but Caesar ignored his ambassadors. Instead, Caesar moved swiftly to the offensive, forced the Pontic king to battle and crushed him – all within five days of arriving in Asia Minor and four hours after first sight of the enemy. Thereafter Caesar wrote to the Senate in Rome *'veni, vidi, vici'* – 'I came, I saw, I conquered'. Later he would remark that Pompey had been fortunate in being able to build a reputation by defeating such feeble enemies.

Caesar then left Asia in a hurry. He pointed out to Mithridates of Pergamon that since Rome ruled Pergamon he was never going to be king of that place, but if Mithridates wanted a kingdom he was welcome to try to take that of Asander – the rebel who had forced Pharnaces to briefly leave off tormenting Domitius Calvinus. Mithridates duly tried, and Asander defeated him in battle. Mithridates, the man who would be king, died either of his wounds or soon thereafter for whatever reason.

Meanwhile, Caesar hastened on to the next phase of his war in Africa, where the defeated Cato Uticensis, who committed suicide rather than submit to his hated enemy. From there Caesar rushed on to Spain, and in March 45 BC he defeated the sons of Pompey at the Battle of Munda and finally wrapped up the civil war. Yet Caesar had still one last battle to fight, and for this confrontation he headed to Rome and the enemy with which he was least equipped to deal – the Roman Senate.

Caesar's other opponents had been military foes, and these he was superbly capable of dispatching. His enemies in the Senate, however, were political and, as has been mentioned previously, Caesar was a lousy politician. Had he been a better politician he would have been able to deal with his other problems earlier instead of being stuck for months in Alexandria dealing with a crisis of his own making. Indeed, a better politician than Caesar would have avoided being dragged into the whole civil war in the first place. So it was probably with considerable discomfort that Caesar settled down to an uneasy tussle with the Senate – a tussle not helped by the arrival of Cleopatra in Rome to press her claim for Caesar's recognition of their son.

It also did not help that, while Caesar was getting into trouble in Egypt, matters in Rome had been spectacularly mismanaged by his second-in-command, Mark Antony. Caesar was reluctant to publicly disavow his prestigious and aristocratic subordinate. Nevertheless, he must certainly have been peeved that throughout the civil war, including between his post-Alexandria campaigns in Africa and Spain, he had needed to periodically drop into Rome to clean up Antony's latest mess.

Perhaps the most egregious problem lay in Antony's inability to separate private from political – a fault which, admittedly, he shared with most of his contemporaries. Nevertheless, it appears that his major reason for frustrating the legislation of a popular politician called Dolabella was that he believed that Dolabella had in the past seduced his wife. (Antony was not above seducing the wives of others, but the Romans famously had a double standard in such matters.) As a result, much-needed legislation on abolishing debt was deadlocked. When the people demonstrated their disapproval in the forum, Antony unleashed the army on them, resulting in hundreds of deaths.

Meanwhile some of the legions that had returned to Italy after Caesar's victory at Pharsalus had not yet been disbanded and were in a truculent mood. News had reached them of Caesar's difficulties in Alexandria and most of the soldiers assumed that their commander was going to perish there. The men were not at all prepared to accept Antony's authority and remained a threat to the general public and to each other as they squabbled among themselves.

Meanwhile, Antony double-crossed the tribune supporting him against Dolabella, and then stood back as a powerless spectator as the two tribunes waged a vicious feud against each other. The situation was fast degenerating into anarchy, with violent disturbances in the capital to the extent that the shrine of the Vestals was looted.

> The more people that died the greater the disturbance created by the survivors. They believed that Caesar [would not return soon because he] was engaged in a difficult war. However when he made a sudden appearance, the people reluctantly became subdued. There was considerable speculation around the city about what Caesar would do to the malefactors whom most

imagined would come to any conceivable bad end. Yet even at this critical stage Caesar followed his usual practice [and issued a general pardon].

(Cassius Dio, *History* 42.33)

Caesar now recognized that he had made a mistake putting Antony in charge and Antony finished the war as a second-in-command who was not actually in command of anything. However, Caesar knew that Antony was one of the few men genuinely loyal to him, and the pair were reconciled shortly before Caesar spectacularly lost his political battle with the Senate by being assassinated in 44 BC.

Needless to say, Caesar's assassination was a disaster for Cleopatra. She hung around in Rome hoping that Caesarion would be recognized as Caesar's heir and would have been greatly disappointed when it turned out that Caesar had chosen instead to posthumously adopt his young relative Octavian rather than the son he had fathered in Alexandria. When Octavian arrived in Rome, Cleopatra returned to Egypt. Rightly assuming that the Romans had more to worry about at that moment than dynastic affairs in Egypt, she killed off her inconvenient brother and co-regent and elevated her son to the throne as Ptolemy XV.

Another Roman civil war followed and when the victorious triumvirs divided the Roman world between them, Octavian took the west and Cleopatra and Egypt became part of the area controlled by Antony. The romance of Antony and Cleopatra is not something we need go into here, other than to mention that Cleopatra did well out of it politically. For a start she was able to get Antony to order the execution of her inconvenient sister Arsinoe in her temple in Ephesus, and she also persuaded Antony to recognize Egypt's claim to various other overseas territories.

With Antony as her latest Roman lover, it appeared that Cleopatra had made the right decision to ally as closely with Rome as she had. Unfortunately, it was that same close connection that Octavian used to turn the Roman people against Antony. Alleging that Cleopatra had corrupted Antony with her decadent Egyptian ways, Octavian used the pretext of declaring war on Cleopatra as a means of forcing Antony into a war against him.

Octavian won his war and became the Emperor Augustus. He took Egypt as a personal possession, rather than make it an imperial province. By then Antony and Cleopatra were dead by suicide, and the only actor remaining from Caesar's time in Alexandria was his son Caesarion. When asked what should become of the boy, Augustus is said to have remarked thoughtfully, 'One can have too many Caesars.' The henchmen of Augustus took the hint, and Caesarion was hunted down and killed.

This left only one character in the drama of Caesar at Alexandria, and that was the city of Alexandria itself. Augustus was by far a better politician than Caesar, and he had the further advantage that the people of the city had learned at first hand the danger of opposing the Roman legions. In fact they had learned it twice, for Antony's last stand at Alexandria had been a bloody one. Octavian took thousands of casualties while trying to wrest the city from Antony – a glimpse, perhaps, of what Caesar might have had to go through had he not galloped directly to Alexandria after his victory on the Nile and seized the city while the defenders were still demoralized by the news of their pharaoh's death.

Like Caesar before him, Augustus did not punish the Alexandrians for being on the wrong side, especially as in the case of Antony the citizens did not really have a choice. From there, Alexandria settled down to become one of the leading cities of the eastern Roman empire. Being Alexandrians, the people did not settle down entirely quietly and the city was rocked with disturbances often enough to necessitate a Roman legion being based in that city rather than in the interior of Egypt as one might have expected.

Despite having been somewhat battered during the early stages of Caesar's stay, the Great Library of Alexandria remained a major centre of learning throughout the early imperial period. It hosted luminaries such as Heron, who demonstrated to the world the first steam engine and the first vending machine (among other inventions) and Galen, among the greatest of ancient physicians.

Today, little sign remains of Caesar's struggle for survival in Alexandria. The Pharos lighthouse has gone, felled by earthquakes in the medieval era. The Heptastadion is no longer needed to link Pharos Island with the mainland as shifting tides and silt accumulation have created two completely separate harbours and Pharos is no longer an island but an oddly-shaped peninsula.

Archaeologists long despaired of finding the royal palace of Cleopatra under the bustling streets of the modern city. Nevertheless, it turned out that the Lachias Peninsula where Caesar stood siege has indeed much to offer modern researchers – once they started looking in the right place. It transpires that much of ancient Alexandria sank beneath the sea during the medieval era as a result of seismic activity and a changing coastline. Archaeologists should have been looking not beneath the streets but beneath the waves.

Now that they have started doing so, literally thousands of artefacts have been discovered as well as ancient streets and the wharves where Caesar's men fought the soldiers of Achillas. Today there is a new battle of Alexandria under way, as archaeologists fight to study the ruins before modern developers build on top of them. In the end it seems that modern progress might do far more damage to the ancient city than Caesar ever did.

Chapter 13

Caesar in Alexandria – the Cultural Fallout

After his defeat of the Alexandrians, Caesar went on to fight and win wars in Africa and Spain. Perhaps unsurprisingly, only one of these wars – the Alexandrian – went on to become the subject of art, theatre and the cinema. Caesar's Spanish war has failed to inspire any great artists, whereas his stay in Egypt has merited the productions of a (generally accurate) play by George Bernard Shaw, an opera by Handel and a mention by William Shakespeare.

The mention by Shakespeare is worth raising because – like many of Shakespeare's expressions – one by Cleopatra has since entered the English language. Shakespeare has Cleopatra refer to her relationship with Caesar as being when she was in 'My salad days, when I was green in judgement' (*Antony and Cleopatra*, 1606–7, act 1, sc. 5, l. 73). Since then the term 'salad days' has moved into general usage to refer to a time when one was young and carefree, if none too wise.

Below follows a brief and non-comprehensive list of later works depicting Caesar in Alexandria – which range from the sublime arias of Graun in 1742 to the ridiculous 1964 *Carry on Cleo* (which features the nevertheless sublime Kenneth Williams as Caesar, and the notorious line 'Infamy! Infamy! They all have it in fer me!').

The reason for the focus on Caesar's Alexandrian adventure is, of course, the power which Cleopatra holds over audiences both ancient and modern. Her ability to take history by the forelock (or in Caesar's case by something lower down) and twist it to favour herself is justly famed. Whether she did this by her voluptuous form – as made explicit in many of the works described below – or by her charming

168 Julius Caesar in Egypt

personality, as the ancient biographer Plutarch believed, or simply – as many modern historians reckon – by shrewd diplomacy and political nous, Cleopatra steals the scene in every historical event in which she is involved.

For an example of voluptuosity, one need look no further than the famous painting usually known today as *Cleopatra before Caesar* by the French Academic artist Jean-Léon Gérôme. This oil-on-canvas painting was executed in 1866. In the painting Cleopatra is both literally and metaphorically before Caesar, who is a somewhat blurry figure wrapped in a red general's cape in the background.

Somehow Gérôme's Cleopatra has emerged beautifully groomed from the carpet in which modern legend insists she was smuggled into the palace. She is shown as a youthful, oriental beauty wearing skimpy harem pants and a totally transparent top. Disregarding the servant crouching at her crotch level, she eyes Caesar like a cat with a particularly succulent mouse.

Cleopatra in the painting owes her aquiline nose to the philosopher Blaise Pascal (1623-1662) who makes the remarkable claim 'That nose of Cleopatra: if it had been shorter, the whole face of the earth would have changed' (Pascal, *Pensées* 162.) There was a current belief that the more prominent the nose, the stronger the character, and Pascal argued that if Cleopatra had not overwhelmed Caesar and Antony by the sheer force of her personality then Augustus might never have come to rule Rome with all the consequences this would bring.

In most depictions of Caesar in Egypt the fact that he was there to fight a brief but remarkably nasty war is treated somewhat as background noise. Where this is mentioned it is because one effect of the war was to put Cleopatra in power – otherwise the military action is generally passed over. The fact that Caesar's life was endangered by his partisan choice to favour Cleopatra over Ptolemy is generally seen as an example of how far Cleopatra was able to sway men from their better judgement.

The number of powerful personalities combined with the exotic background of Egypt persuaded Handel to produce his famous *Julius Caesar in Egypt* – which is still regarded today as one of the finest baroque operas. The opera is roughly based upon the actual events, but even more upon an earlier libretto of 1676 with music by one Antonio Sartorio. While the Egyptian general Achillas is sung by a bass, for some reason Handel opted for the notoriously over-sexed Caesar to be sung castrato.

Cleopatra is a soprano who informs Caesar in the aria *Tu la mia stella sei* 'You are my star, my lovely hope who furnishes my desires with gratitude and pleasure.' Exactly what the writer of the *Alexandrine War* would have made of this production one can only speculate.

A later opera in 1742 was commissioned for the Prussian leader Frederick the Great to commemorate the opening of his court opera house. Again the language of the opera, by Carl Heinrich Graun, was in Italian with the libretto composed by Bottarelli, though a German translation soon followed. Yet again Caesar was sung castrato. The plot, with its full-blooded characters who throw themselves into the action with whole-hearted and ill-considered abandon makes for a thoroughly enjoyable experience.

The play by George Bernard Shaw presents an altogether more childish Cleopatra:

> I am the Queen; and I shall live in the palace at Alexandria when I have killed my brother, who drove me out of it. When I am old enough I shall do just what I like. I shall be able to poison the slaves and see them wriggle.'

But the intent is to show Caesar in the light of the British colonial experience, of which Shaw did not greatly approve.

While earlier productions of the modern age showed Caesar and Cleopatra as mostly driven by their hormones, Shaw steps back to the writers of the Classical era and adds a dash of cool realpolitik to the famed love affair and also takes more than a passing interest in the war going on in the background. The play was particularly relevant to Shaw as the British of his day were attempting to follow in Caesar's footsteps and establish their rule over Egypt through proxy rulers. (The British later switched to direct rule which lasted until 1956.)

The arrival of cinema inspired several producers to take a shot at telling the story of Caesar in Egypt. The award for the most opulent of these productions must go to the 1963 production *Cleopatra*, which starred Elizabeth Taylor. Critics rather liked Rex Harrison in his role as Caesar, a role which gave him some memorable lines. These include his description of Cleopatra as 'a descendant of generations of inbred, incestuous, mental defectives'. Unlike some later productions, the script writers had done their homework, and this shows in lines such as Harrison's Caesar declaiming irritably at one point, 'Daughter of an idiotic flute-playing drunkard who bribed his way to the throne of Egypt'. Well, yes.

Harrison's Caesar also makes a valid point about military events in Alexandria: 'There is no such thing as an unimportant war.'

The film made record amounts at the box office, but overall it lost money due to the sheer extravagance of the production. Cleopatra would have approved.

In fact, films featuring Caesar and Cleopatra seem to have simultaneously done reasonably well at the box office and badly in terms of profit. An earlier British production of *Caesar and Cleopatra* managed to capture the wartime ambience rather well, mainly because at the time Britain was at war with Nazi Germany – at one point the director was nearly blown out of his seat when a bomb landed 150 yards away. It did not help that actors had to wear clothing designed to depict the Egyptian summer in a poorly-heated British studio in winter.

Vivian Leigh as Cleopatra was suffering from considerable mental and physical stress at the time, and this detracted from the kittenish minx she was supposed to be playing. She was pregnant in the early scenes then slipped on a floor in one scene which caused her to tragically miscarry the baby she desperately wanted. Even the efforts of Claude Raines as Caesar did not stop some early reviews from labelling the production as 'a stinker'. The film cost the studio £3,000,000 – a fortune at the time.

One of the latest productions to feature Caesar in Alexandria is a 2002 film called *Mission Cleopatra*. Given that this is based on an earlier animated film which was in turn drawn (literally) from the famous Asterix the Gaul cartoons, one must enjoy the film and observations of the characters without worrying much, or at all, about historical accuracy (although, in a nod to Pascal, everyone remarks that Cleopatra 'has a cute nose').

Before we finish this far from comprehensive survey it is also worth mentioning *Caesar meeting Cleopatra* painted in 1747 by Giovanni Domenico Tiepolo. Tiepolo enjoyed painting scenes from ancient history, and this combination of powerful characters in an evocative setting was clearly more than he could resist.

From the above it may be seen that Cleopatra and her love life have taken almost all the attention given by the modern world to Caesar's Alexandrian adventure. Even here in this appendix, the lure of the Egyptian queen has ultimately proven too strong to resist. However, it is to be hoped that elsewhere this text has moved the spotlight back to where it properly belongs – to the heroic Roman soldiers who defended the Lachias Peninsula against overwhelming odds.

Above all, credit goes to the men of Caesar's Sixth legion, whose unflagging loyalty and grim determination in even the bleakest of circumstances makes one wish that they had died bravely for a better cause.

Index

Achaea, 37
Achillas, 40, 42, 43, 47, 53, 54, 71, 73–7, 90, 124, 166, 169
Aegean Sea, 17
Aegyptus (founding father), 21
Africa, 8, 11, 12, 18, 34, 44, 62, 82, 116, 159, 160, 162, 163, 167
Ahenobarbus, Domitius, 5
Alban Hills, 44
Alesia, 36, 113, 128, 129
Alexander the Great, 15, 16, 18, 21, 35, 60–3, 65, 124, 125, 159
Alexandria, 1, 8–13, 15–18, 21–4, 26, 27, 35, 37–9, 45–50, 57, 58, 60–6, 69, 70, 72, 73, 75–7, 79, 81–4, 87–91, 93, 100, 105–107, 116, 117, 120–7, 129, 131, 132, 134, 135, 138, 139, 141, 143, 144, 146, 152, 154, 159, 160–7, 169–71
Alexandriae, 61
Alexandrine War, *see* referenced texts
Alveus Steganus channel, 93
Anatolia, 10, 11, 82, 121, 161
Antioch, 59
Antipater the Idumean, 126, 132, 144
Antirhodos harbour, 72, 78
Antony, Mark, 33, 39, 51, 60, 159, 162–5, 167, 168
Arabian Gulf, 62
Arsaces, king, 12
Arsinoe, 19, 26, 40, 47, 54, 66, 77, 84, 115–19, 124, 153, 158, 164
Asander, 162
Asia, 18
  Minor, viii, 4, 11, 31, 35, 38, 43, 54, 75, 82, 119, 120, 133, 158–62
  Province of, 37

Asterix, 171
Athens, 17, 60
Atticus, Pomponius, 160
Augustus, 71, 122, 165, 168
  see also Octavian

Babylon, 62, 65
Berenice, daughter of Auletes, 24
Bithynia, 51
Bottarelli, 169
Britain, 72, 170

Caecilii Metelli, 29
  see also Metellus
Caesarion (Ptolemy XV), 59, 160, 164, 165
Cairo, 131
Caligula, emperor, 138
Calvinus, Domitius, 81–4, 88, 161, 162
Canopus, 122
Canopus Decree, 18
Capitoline Hill, 158
Carfulenus, Decimus, 149
Carthage, 20
Cassius, Gaius, 45, 54
Cato Uticensis, 9, 11, 34, 82, 162
Cenabum (Orleans), 36
Cicero, Marcus Tullius, 27, 29, 59, 159, 160
Cilicia, 10, 48, 121
cisterns, 63, 77
Claudia, gens, 122
Claudius, 122
Cleopatra, Berenice, 22, 23
Cleopatra II of Macedon, 21
  sister of Alexander, 21

the Danaid, 21
wife of Ptolemy V, 21
Cleopatra II of Egypt, 21
Cleopatra III of Egypt, 21, 22
Cleopatra V of Egypt, 23
Cleopatra VII, viii–x, xii, 23, 25, 26, 35, 40, 41, 47–55, 59, 60, 65, 66, 71, 77, 115–18, 121, 124, 125, 127, 145, 153, 157–60, 162, 164–71
Corcyra, 11
Corinth, 126
Cornelia, 43, 44
Crassus, Marcus Licinius, 12, 31
Crete, 72
Cyprus, 17, 24, 39, 158
Cyrenaica, 13, 17

Damascus, 16
Danaids, 21
David, king, 145
Dinocrates, 63
Dioscorides, 127, 128
Dolabella, 163
Dyrrhachium, 3, 4, 139

Enipeus River, 4, 6
Ephesus, 158, 164
Epirus, 21
Eratosthenes, 17
etesian winds, 45
Ethiopia, 159
Euclid, 17
Euergetes, 18
Eunostos harbour, 64, 93–6, 99–102, 104, 106, 109, 111, 122
Euphranor the Rhodian, 96, 122, 123, 128
Euphrates river, 12
Europe, 8, 43

Frederick the Great, 169

Gabinians, 26, 42, 48, 51, 73, 102, 145, 152
Gabinius, Aulus, 24, 26, 44, 48, 51, 67, 145
Galatia, 121

Galen, 166
Ganymedes, 77, 78, 84, 89, 90, 116, 117, 119, 120, 153
Gaul, xii, 31, 32, 34, 58, 71, 131, 138
 Cisalpine, 33, 36
Gaza, 13, 36, 39, 74
Germany, 137, 170
Gérôme, Jean-Léon, 168
Graun, Carl Heinrich, 167, 169
Great Harbour, 64, 88, 89, 93–5, 100, 104, 105, 111
Greece, 3, 4, 10, 33, 34, 36, 38, 62, 71–3, 126, 161

Hadrian, emperor, 122
Handel, 167, 169
Hannibal, 19
Harrison, Rex, 170
Heptastadion, 64, 65, 89, 93–5, 98–100, 104–108, 110, 111, 113, 115, 166
Herod, king, 138, 144
Heron, 166
Himalayas, 62
Hirtius, Aulus, 9, 10, 59
 see also Alexandrine War
Horatius Cocles, 100, 105

Ides of March, 45
India, 18, 62, 159
Iskandar, 60
 see also Alexander
Italy, 2–4, 11, 25, 31–4, 38, 45, 116, 163

Judea, 138
Julia, daughter of Caesar, 160
Julia gens, 160
Julio-Claudian dynasty, 122

Kandahar, Afghanistan, 60
Kibotus quay, 94
kleroi, 146

Lachias Peninsula, 64, 72–4, 83, 84, 93, 99, 112, 113, 128, 134, 135, 143, 149, 150, 155, 166, 171

Legio,
  VI Hispaniensis, 36, 37, 102, 103, 110, 113, 138, 139, 143, 149, 150, 161, 171
  XXVII, 82, 143, 161
  XXVIII, 37, 113
Leigh, Vivian, 170
Lesbos, 10
Levant, the, 16, 31, 126, 144
Levantine seaboard, 73
Lollia, wife of Gabinius, 51
Lucullus, Licinius, 11
Lycia, 75

Maccabees, 144
Macedon/Macedonia, 10, 20, 22, 34, 61, 65
Magas Ptolemy, 19
Mareotis, lake, 63, 77
Marius, Caius, 28, 29, 59
Memphis, 61, 127, 159
Metelli gens, 30
Metellus Pius, 29, 30
misthophoroi, 145
Mithridates VI Eupator (the Great), 1, 82, 120, 121, 161
Mithridates of Pergamum, 120, 121, 124–9, 131–7, 143, 144, 161, 162
Munda, Battle of, 162
Mutina, Battle of, 60
Mytilene, 10

Nabatea, 72
Nero, *see* Tiberius
Nicomedes of Bithynia, king, 51
Nile, river, 16, 25, 39, 57, 61, 62, 73, 76, 100, 122, 123, 131, 132, 134, 135, 137, 139–42, 148, 149, 152, 153, 158, 160, 165

Octavian, 59, 164, 165
  see also Augustus
Oppius, Gaius, 57–9
Oppius/Hirtius, 60
Orleans/Cenabum, 36
Ostia, 1

Parthia, 12, 13
Pascal, Blaise, 168, 171
Peloponnese, 126
Peloponnesian War, 85
Pelusium, 39, 41, 43, 124–7, 144
Per-Amun, 39
Pergamon, 72, 75, 162
Pericles, 17
Perpenna, Marcus, 2
Persian,
  Gulf, 62
  Units, 145
Pharnaces II, viii, 11, 82, 161, 162
Pharos, isle and Lighthouse, 64, 75, 81, 89, 93–106, 110–12, 143, 166
Pharsalus, Battle of, x, 4, 10, 11, 13, 26, 31, 34–7, 45, 73, 82, 86, 113, 144, 145, 160, 163
Philip II of Macedon, 21
Philip V of Macedon, 10
Plutarch, 3, 6, 10, 12, 28, 29, 41, 43, 49, 50, 51, 53, 59, 110, 168
Pompeius Magnus, *see* below
Pompey, Gnaeus, 1–10, 12, 13, 15, 24–7, 31–47, 53, 54, 59, 66, 67, 69, 73, 81, 82, 121, 124, 125, 144, 145, 160, 162
Pompey Sextus, 11
Pontifex Maximus, 5, 29
Poseidon, 94, 95, 98
Pothinus, 40, 41, 47, 48, 53, 71
Ptolemaic dynasty/Ptolemies, 15, 17–23, 25, 39, 40, 60, 62–5, 71, 77, 114, 115, 127, 145
  Ptolemy I Soter, 16–18, 65, 71, 127
  Ptolemy II Philadelphus, 17, 18
  Ptolemy III Euergetes, 18, 19
  Ptolemy IV Philopater, 19
  Ptolemy V Epiphanes, 20, 21
  Ptolemy VI, 21
  Ptolemy VII, 21
  Ptolemy VIII, 21, 65
  Ptolemy IX, 23
  Ptolemy X, 22–4
  Ptolemy XI, 22, 23
  Ptolemy XII Auletes, 12, 23–5, 39, 40, 41, 52, 53, 70, 157
  Ptolemy XIII, viii, 12, 25, 26, 35, 39–44, 47–9, 52–5, 59, 65, 66, 70,

77, 81, 115–21, 124, 125, 127, 128, 131, 132, 134–7, 140–9, 151–3, 168
Ptolemy XIV, 157, 164
Ptolemy XV, 164
  see also Caesarion
Pyramid, Great at Giza, 64

Rabirius, Gaius, 25
Raines, Claude, 171
Ramesses II, 16, 127
Raphia, Battle of, 19
Rhakontis, 61, 65
Rhodes, 37, 85
Roman Republic, viii, xiii, 33, 34, 66, 69, 70, 116, 160
Rome, 1, 2, 4, 8, 10, 11, 12, 13, 15, 20, 22, 23, 25, 27–33, 35, 36, 40, 41, 44–6, 52, 59, 60, 61, 66, 69, 70, 82, 112, 118, 122, 137–9, 145, 157, 158, 160–4, 168
Rosetta Stone, 19
Rubicon, the, 25, 33, 38, 59, 139

Salvius, centurion, 42, 43
Sartorio, Antonio, 169
Scipio, 5
  Africanus, 59
Seleucid, 1, 18, 22, 124, 144
Septimus, tribune, 42
Sertorius, Quintus, 1, 2
Shakespeare, William, 50, 167
Shaw, George Bernard, 167, 169, 170
Sinai, the, 26
Sosimus, 19
Spain, 1, 2, 11, 12, 30, 31, 34, 36, 82, 113, 116, 159, 160, 162, 163, 167
Sulla, Lucius Cornelius, 28, 29
Syria, 1, 12, 26, 39, 48, 115, 121

Taylor, Elizabeth, 170
Tempe, Vale of, 10
Tencteri, 138
thalamegos, 159
Thames, river, 72
Theodotus of Chios, 40–2, 48, 53
Thessaly, 4, 10, 35, 37, 73
Tiber, river, 110
Tiberius Nero, 122–4

Tiberius (emperor), 122
Tiepolo, Giovanni Domenico, 171
Tigranes of Armenia, 11
Tivoli, 122
triumvirs/triumvirate, 12, 31, 41, 47, 164
Troy, 27
Tunisia, 11
Tyre, 18, 62

Venus, goddess, 27
Vercingetorix, 12, 36, 128, 129, 131, 139, 158
Vestals, shrine of, 163
Vitellius, Emperor, 46

Wellington, Duke of, 111, 112
Williams, Kenneth, 167

Writers and texts
Aeschylus, *The Suppliants*, 21
Appian, xi
  Civil Wars, 109, 119, 158
  Spanish War, 59

Belov, A., *Navigational aspects of calling to the Great Harbour of Alexandria*, 93

Caesar, *De Bello Gallico*, 58
Cassius Dio, *History*, x, 10, 11, 35, 44, 47, 50, 123, 132, 133, 150, 164
Cicero, *Epistulae Ad Atticum*, 160

Florus, *Epitome*, 153

Hirtius, *De Bello Alexandrino (Alexandrine War)*, vii–x, 36, 57–60, 67, 75, 76, 79, 85, 90, 96, 98, 99, 114, 117, 118, 123, 127, 131–3, 138, 140, 146, 149, 150

Josephus, xi, 132
  Antiquities, 126

Suetonius, *Caesar*, 32, 57, 58, 109, 157, 158
  Tiberius, 124